S

Asian

Martial

Arts

- cambodia
- myanmar
- thailand
- vietnam

An Anthology of Articles from the *Journal of Asian Martial Arts*

Compiled by Michael A. DeMarco, M.A.

Copyright © 2017
by Via Media Publishing Company
941 Calle Mejia #822, Santa Fe, NM 87501 USA

Articles in this anthology
were originally published in the
Journal of Asian Martial Arts.
Listed according to the table
of contents for this anthology:

Allan, D. (2002), Vol. 11 No. 3, pp. 40-49
Skaggs, J. (2003), Vol. 12 No. 4, pp. 48-65
Tran, J. (2004), Vol. 13 No. 2, pp. 64-79
Mallon, S. (2005), Vol. 14 No. 2, pp. 30-43
Loh, H. L. (2011), Vol. 20 No. 3, pp. 32-37
Winborne, D. (2014), Vol. 23, pp. 14-36

Book and cover design by
Via Media Publishing Company

Edited by
Michael A. DeMarco, M.A.

Cover illustration

Kickboxer courtesy of Shutterstock.com
Stock photo ID: 170702366

ISBN 978-1-893765-45-0

contents

preface

What martial arts are associated with Thailand, Vietnam, Cambodia, and Myanmar (Burma)? What makes them unique when compared with other Asian martial systems? This anthology is a convenient collection that focuses on the martial arts of these areas, such as the familiar art of Muay Thai, and lesser-known arts of Than Quyen of Vietnam, Burmese bando, and Cambodian leth wei.

In chapter one, the David Allan brings readers inside the Lumphini Stadium in Bangkok to witness the fighters' kickboxing skills and etiquette through text and photographs. He also records how musicians play and the locals participate in each event, with emotional exuberance of cheering, and betting.

Jeremy Skaggs wanted to go to Thailand to train with some of the top Muay Thai fighters. His chapter allows readers to relive his experience through text and superb photography. He reports on his travel to Thailand, daily training routines, daily life there, and a night at the Lumphini Stadium.

Chapter three by Jason Tran presents the origin and functions of That Son Than Quyen's "spirit forms" as inspired by real and mythic animals. This is accomplished by contrasting Than Quyen with Chinese imitation styles, tracing the development of Vietnam religion and superstitions, and exploring the impact of geographic and cultural elements.

In the next chapter Scott Mallon recounts excursions he made into Myanmar and Cambodia to learn about their indigenous martial arts firsthand. He reports on the Muay Thai-like systems and their similarities and difference, along with the special cultural atmospheres where these arts are found. Excellent photo coverage highlight the martial artists.

Loh Han Loong's chapter goes beyond the common views of Thai boxing by critically examining the way Muay Thai is portrayed in nonacademic sources, such as articles and websites. The manner in which Muay Thai is framed in popular culture is not simply the result of historical facts, but is a way of creating the Thai nation myth and the uniqueness of Thai culture.

The lengthy final chapter by Dr. Winborne focuses on the bando system. His chapter explores ancient Burmese fighting traditions and their evolution to modern-day martial arts practices. Bando is a seamless amalgam of striking methods, grappling techniques, weapons approaches, and healing strategies from the Southeast Asian country currently known as Myanmar. This comprehensive self-defense system is reviewed and analyzed based on documented viewpoints of prominent masters and practitioners. The philosophy and principles that undergird the bando system are discussed as well.

This anthology offers a concise overview of the history, cultures, and combative systems associated with the geographic areas of Cambodia, Myanmar, Vietman, and Thailand. Familiar or not with these martial traditions, readers will be find the chapters informative and photography delightful.

Michael A. DeMarco, Publisher
Santa Fe, New Mexico
March 2017

chapter 1

Two Boys Enter, Two Men Leave:
A Night in Bangkok's Kickboxing Thunderdome

by David G. Allan

All photographs courtesy of David G. Allan.

Lumphini Statium, Bangkok — It's a Tuesday night. Inexplicably the best night for Muay Thai at this, the older, smokier, and by all accounts better, of Bangkok's two kickboxing crucibles.

On this night it is even more crowded than usual as the caliber of fighters is all main event-worthy in their weight classes. Not a single ringside seat is free. All the expensive seats are taken up by *farang* (foreigners)—tourists suckered into purchasing the inflatedly priced chairs but who would never admit they were snookered. Behind me is standing room only—all Thai men, mostly betting at a stock-exchange-floor frenzy and yelling at every side blow, "Yayh!" My Thai is poor so I asked a native speaker what they were shouting. "Nothing," she said, "It's just yelling."

On a typical night there are five major events, with a couple of preliminary matches at the start and a few lesser bouts after the main event. If you're unfamiliar with Thai kickboxing, considered by many to be the toughest of the martial arts, it is an endurance test that allows fighters to use any part of their body (except the head) to hit any part of their opponent. Unlike boxing, which can run out a lot of time on the clock with footwork and energy-conserving jabs, the Muay Thai action is nonstop. Because kickboxing is much faster paced than its Western counterpart, matches last only five rounds of three minutes each, with a two-minute break between each round.

Where I sit, in the middle section, it's a beltway of dirty wooden benches cut into a polygonal shape around the ring, protected from the out-of-towners in front and the wildly betting Thais behind by metal fencing. In front of me sits the band, blowing out the bagpipe-sounding squeals of the *pii chawaa* (Thai oboe) and banging the *glong kaek* drum faster and faster to match the action in the ring.

Even in mid-February the heat would be unbearable with so many bodies in this circus tent-shaped building without the fans spinning from the corrugated roof ceiling. The stadium is very "Frank Gehry", my friend Kami tells me, all fence and metal. Gehry should visit this place and see his vision in all its pulsing, banging, sweaty Thai-ness. This is where architecture and blood mix and Lumphini (unlike its large concrete sister Ratchadamnoen Stadium) looks as if it might shake down like a pile of Lincoln Logs under the jostling weight of the excited crowd. This is sport in its best possible incarnation—no commercial breaks, no commentary, no replays. The music is live, the action is spitting distance away, and no one is getting up for a hot dog. In Thailand, it's the best show going.

The First Event

Two preteens enter the ring. They are mini-flyweights at 102 pounds each, and have pecks and washboard stomachs that would make you confuse them with adult pygmies, not 11-year-olds.

Before a Muay Thai fight begins, each boxer performs a ritualistic dance called the *ram muay*, a slow and serious tribute to their training camp and coach which incorporates moves to please the spirits and draw power from the four elements. Every boxer's moves are similar, but the order and length of the ceremony is individually designed and practiced. The rhythmic ceremony, lasting about five minutes, includes patterned moves such as outstretched or rotating arms and bouncing on one's knee. The tradition dates back to a time when Muay Thai was fought outside and the low-to-the-ground movement helped the fighters size up the condition of the dirt circle (back when a ring was really a ring and not a box). All *ram muay* ceremonies include a special bow, or *wai kru*, given to the trainer (*kru*, "teacher"), as well as turning to the four corners of the ring in recognition of the four noble truths of the Buddha: compassion, temperance, prudence and justice. The solemn ritual is graceful in its religious and symbolic earnestness and a fascinating extension of a sport that has the distinction of originating in a Buddhist country.

At the end of ram muay the fighter walks counterclockwise around the ring running his gloved hand over the top rope to dispel the bad spirits that can cause defeat. Around the fighters' biceps are *kruang rang* amulets—cords containing lucky herbs or Buddhist amulets, worn for protection. Around his head is a *monkhon*, a stiff, monk-blessed headband marking his camp, and while the *kruang rang* will remain worn during the match, the monkhon is removed after the opening ceremony. And just before the match begins, the fighter *wais* (bows) three times: once for Buddha, once for the *sangha* (order of monks) and once for the Buddhist Dharma (Doctrine).

Back in the ring Toy Ting, in the red corner, has breezed through his ram muay quickly and is getting a rub down by his trainer, who spits water on his legs and kneads his flesh. Manee Paeng, in the blue corner, continues with his slow dance and wais, unhurried and focused in a meditative concentration being watched by his opponent.

Throughout their match Toy goes for too much, exerting energy on attempts to trip or grab Manee's arms. But Manee has none of it and holds firm and balanced, waiting for his opportunities without fear or expression. The match is slow by Muay Thai standards but Manee wins and it seems to me that his concentration, from ritual through the final bell, was his greatest ally.

Muay Thai fighters begin their training as young as age six and often retire in their mid-20s. Sent off at a young age to live in one of the nearly 100 Muay Thai camps (a tradition that began in the early 1600s), many boxers will change their last names to the name of their training center out of love and pride. The boxers are surprisingly well paid (on the high end, 100,000 baht, or $2,300 a match), one of the few opportunities a poor family in Thailand has for sudden wealth. Many of Thailand's best fighters have come from the impoverished northeast region of the country where scouts are often sent to find tough, athletic youngsters working on farms. Once accepted into a camp, the boy will be blessed by a monk and given his *kruang rang*.

3

The Second Event

Yodsaenglai versus the Thai uncommonly-named David. I'm rooting for my namesake but the crowd is with the more imposing and severe Yodsaenglai, the returning champion. The crowd was right. David takes an early punishment and doesn't seem to understand my English pleas to "Hang in there!"

Yodsaenglai easily wins the first two rounds, holding up his hands in a common post-round sign of victory. David's cabal of trainers are taking turns barking advice to him and he nods at everything they say. And then, at the start of round three, it starts to turn and David begins a serious comeback. An unprepared Yodsaenglai is soon on the ropes and David is blocking kicks and uppercutting his opponent's scowling face with great speed. Yodsaenglai continues to fight hard and at the end of the third round grabs David's legs and starts punching him—a move that isn't against the rules but seems harsh, desperate, and finds little favor from the crowd. By the fourth round the excited spectators are with the underdog and David is loudly cheered on as he makes impressive kicking leaps at Yodsaenglai's head. The live music has picked up an equally furious pace and every "ching" of the band's tiny cymbals brings a blow from one side or the other.

The ringside Phipat band, consisting of a *pee chawaa* horn, two *glong kaek* bongo drums and the donut-sized, onomatopoeically-named *ching* bronze symbols, plays the tune that is standard for all Muay Thai matches. The *wong pee glong* music starts off with a slow and soft composition during the pre-fight ceremony and then picks up with a quick-tempo composition once the fighting begins, increasing its pace and volume as the match progresses.

By the final round of the match between David and Yodsaenglai, the music runs at a fast clanging heart rate of 200 beats a minute with both pugilists also at full throttle. By the time the final bell rings the whole stadium is yelling and both fighters look exhausted. There is a long pause while the referee confers with the three judges before lifting David's hand in victory. Yodsaenglai falls to his knees and bows to David. They hug and smile and thank each others' trainers, who in turn present each boy a garland of flowers around his neck. It is very un-Thai to embarrass your opponent, so once the fighting is over everyone is friends, no matter how intense the match.

The Third Event

Several sanctioned gofers in the audience wait for you to finish your beer to see if you want another. I asked for a *Chang* (a beer of malt liquor degree, produced by Carlsberg but given a Thai name—*chang* means elephant —to sell to a nationalist population) and it arrives before the fight begins. The third event consists of the night's heaviest fighters, weighing in at 133 pounds and looking like Muay Thai oldtimers in their early 20s.

The match heats up in the usual dance of sidekicks, roundhouse jabs, one-two's, and chest kicks. The rounds go quickly. After the action of the last match, the crowd is tamer. The most exciting moment comes when the boxer in red trunks grabs his opponent's head and pushes it down into his upward thrusting knee—a perfectly legal and high-scoring move. While the normal spectators begin to start talking to each other again, only the gamblers are paying close attention. Red wins and the next two fighters are quickly brought in and examined by the bettors.

Betting is the sport-within-a-sport at Muay Thai. It's nearly as fascinating to watch as the fight itself. The bettors shout, pace around, and refuse to blink during the action. Between rounds they throw fingers in the air and make bets across aisles to other bettors in a secret language of digits and odds-making.

All betting is done in the stadium among the bettors themselves, so neither the house nor the fighters get a cut. Every bet is made with just one other person for agreed-upon amounts and odds and every bet is remembered and paid later. You could make dozens of bets with dozens of other bettors at varying amounts and odds and you'd have to recall all of it in order to pay, or be paid, at the end of the night. To further confuse things, betting can take place anytime during the match, so the odds are constantly changing as the fight progresses.

The wagering usually begins to take on a frantic pace between the third and fourth rounds. But the odds-making begins from the opening ram muay ceremony, when the bettors will size up the fighters, taking into account the integrity with which they perform their ritual dance—like racetrack regulars who visit the stable before the races. Only the fighters themselves seem to take the fighting more seriously than the gamblers.

Because the whole betting process works on the honor system and not through a state-sponsored entity, Muay Thai stadiums are the one place where former criminals are free to gamble. But what's to keep someone from skipping out on a big loss in all the post-match mayhem, considering the gentlemanly nature of the wagering? I asked a Thai woman who once covered the sport for her college newspaper, and she explained that the stadium will eventually catch the welcher, bring him into a room and strip him down. I thought she was about to tell me they beat the guy up or break his fingers mob-style, but no, they take a Polaroid of him in his underwear and put his picture up on a wall in the office. In a country that puts such a high value on saving face, that's all it takes to keep him from ever returning, she explained.

The Fourth Event

The action of the fourth event is immediately intense. Jumping kicks, rope-a-dope flurries, jabs spraying sweat off the opponent's head—all flow into each other without a break in the action. Squint your eyes and it actually becomes beautiful, divinely coordinated. The bettors are going crazy after just the first round. The second round has the whole stadium yelling "Eeehs!" with every frenzied knee-to-abdomen kick. And Ban Pot in the blue trunks starts to bleed.

The fighters grow more intense with each round. The middle section joins the bettors in standing. Ban Pot's trainers clean him off after each round, but the blood flows faster and faster as successive hits further open the wound. There is no stopping the match for cuts, so both sides become increasingly painted with Ban Pot's blood. The fighters look fierce. The blood flow makes the sport look dangerous and deadly. And the entire stadium has caught the bettors' fever of mad cheering.

Covered in his opponent's blood, red takes the win. The fierceness drains from both fighters as they hug each other and bow to each other's trainers. The drama is over, but the bettors are recounting the action to each other in chatty Thai, grins all around.

Thailand's national sport traces its history back to the *Ramayana*, a Hindu story of good vs. evil depicted in many Thai temples. The sport's moves and stances are actually derived from fights detailed in the epic. The first written mention of Muay Thai dates back to 1411, in Burmese accounts of fighting their neighbors and the Thais' use of a ferocious style of unarmed combat. One account tells the story of Nai Knanom Tom, a Thai prisoner of war and the first known kickboxer, who escaped his Burmese captors by defeating dozens of Burmese warriors. Later, King Naresuan (1590-1605) made it a compulsory skill for military training.

Due to a high injury and death rate, the sport was actually banned in Thailand in the 1920s, only to reenter the ring in 1937 with a new set of rules designed to protect the fighters from debilitating injury—like the banning of glass-impregnated hemp or horse hide gloves.

The Main Event

An announcer enters the ring for the main event and says in Thai what I imagine to be, "In the blue conaaa, weighing in at 131 pounds, the heavyweight from the Giat Wanlop camp… Noooontaaachai! And in the red conaa … sporting Batman symbol shorts, also weighing in at 131 pounds, from the Giat Monthep camp… Saaaaaaam Goooooor!"

Unlike other Asian martial arts, Muay Thai training is grueling and requires full contact sparring. Most camps have regimented schedules and special diets for their fighters as well. No other martial artist has ever defeated a ranking *nak muay* (Muay Thai fighter). Hong Kong once staged matches between its top five kung fu fighters and Bangkok's top kickboxer and lost all five matches in under seven minutes each.

While many Muay Thai matches are held throughout the country, Lumphini and Ratchadamnoen host the best and there are matches there every day of the year. If you want to see a pre-1937 Queensland Rules Muay Thai match, try to visit Thailand during the annual water festival, Songkran, in April and head to the Thai-Burmese border town of Mae Sot. There a Thai fighter annually challenges a Burmese fighter to a no-rules, hemp-fisted Muay Thai fight in a traditional dirt circle, a fight that ends only after blood has been shed.

Muay Thai fighters will always, given the opportunity, strike with their leg or knee instead of punching their opponent. Punching is considered a weak move and often fails to elicit the reaction of pain that is required in order to score a point. A kick or elbow to the head is preferable. And while there is nothing to prevent groin kicks, that move is avoided. The only tactics not allowed are biting and head-butting. Also, grappling and holding your opponent while knees to the ribs are exchanged is not immediately broken-up by the referee. Sometimes the boxers are permitted to hold each other for minutes, often against the ropes.

Most ring fights will go the distance of all five rounds, but occasionally there is a knockout. On an off night, during a preliminary fight of newbies, I saw a "knockout" of one scared youngster, where he clearly went down to end the match (he actually helped the trainers get himself on the stretcher), but I've also seen the real thing.

As the main event began, the two headliners danced around each other, looking for an opportunity for their first strike. After a night of long, intense and bloody fighting, the stadium crowd was set for five full rounds of action. After a minute of easy sparring, Saam Gor, in his Batman logo shorts, spun around hitting Nontachai in the head with his shin and knocking him out cold—a spectacular conclusion to an exceptionally great night of Muay Thai.

chapter 2

Daily Life at a Muay Thai
Boxing Camp in Phetburi

by Jeremy Skaggs, B.A.

Photography by Jeremy Skaggs.

Introduction

Muay Thai is not only one of the most brutal fighting styles in the world, it is a significant part of Thai culture. Its origins go back hundreds of years when the Thai (Siamese) armies used it to defend their borders against foreign invaders. Aside from Buddhism, Muay Thai has linked every class of Thai society together, being practiced by great kings as well as poor farm boys.

Despite its importance to the Thai people, the ancient martial art was banned in 1927 due to its high injury and death rates. But in 1938, Muay Thai reemerged as a sport, complete with safety rules and protective equipment for the fighters to wear. Bouts were now fought in rings, with a referee to enforce the rules and control the action of the fight. Thailand now has over 60,000 professional boxers, and the sport's popularity has spread throughout much of the world.

I first became interested in Muay Thai about six years ago when a gym opened in my hometown of Louisville, Kentucky. I was a boxer and full-contact karate fighter at the time, but I decided to quit what I was doing to train in Muay Thai. After my first day of training, I realized that it was more challenging than it looked and was also the hardest thing I had ever done.

Over the next few years, I traveled with our team and fought whenever I got the chance. Although I had won nearly all of my boxing and full-contact karate bouts, my success in Muay Thai was mixed. The sport is so competitive than even the best Muay Thai fighters in the world have many loses on their records and retire from the sport in their early twenties. I was already in my twenties when I started, so I knew I would not be able to fight for very long.

Three years and ten fights later, I decided it was time for me to quit and move on with my career in photojournalism. But I never lost my love for the sport or my interest in Asian culture. I had always wanted to go to Thailand and train with some of the best fighters in the world and watch the fights at Lumphini Stadium. And being a photographer, I wanted to document my experience on film, combining my two biggest passions.

In Thailand, Muay Thai fighters live and train at boxing camps scattered throughout the country. They usually come from poor underprivileged families and fight to earn money to send back to their parents and to make a better life for themselves. The other boys at the camp become their new family and Muay Thai becomes their way of life.

Travel to Thailand

It is becoming increasingly popular for Muay Thai fighters from many other countries to make the trek to Thailand to train with the Thais. The fighters get a chance to further develop their skills while the Muay Thai camps earn extra money teaching them. The cost is minimal by European and American standards. The average cost for a month's stay, including room and board, is about $500.00 U.S.

There are still camps that are very traditional and do not train foreigners. Most of these are outside of Bangkok in small villages. If you want to see Muay Thai in its purest form with little Western influence, these are the types of camps you want to visit. And this was the type of camp I wanted for my documentary. The problem would be to convince the camp to allow me to stay with them to work on my project. I had no idea it would take me several weeks to find the right place for me to do my work as well as have the chance to train.

I arrived in Bangkok about 11 p.m. on a hot Tuesday night in February. I had left 20 degree Fahrenheit weather in Louisville to be hit by a wall of warm polluted air when I got off my plane. I was a little nervous about being there, but I was also very excited about training at a Muay Thai camp, watching the fights, and seeing an amazing and beautiful country.

11

I spent the first two weeks of my trip traveling around the provinces surrounding Bangkok, when I finally discovered the small rural town of Phetburi. The town sits in a valley surrounded by hills that support an old palace and temple complex that was built 150 years ago by King Rama V. who had used the palace as his summer home. The town below was first settled in the 11th century and eventually became an important trading and cultural center. Phetburi is rich in Thai history, culture, and beauty.

As soon as I got off the bus, I looked for a taxi. Because the town is so small, with very few foreign visitors, the taxis are all small motorcycles. I handed my driver a note that said in Thai, "Can you take me to a boxing camp?" He started talking with a few other guys and one of them gave him directions. He then motioned for me to get on the back of his bike and we took off.

As we rode to the outskirts of the town, I was starting to get a little nervous. I had no idea where this guy was taking me. And I was also concerned that the camp he was taking me to may not be what I was expecting, or that they might not accept me. I was hoping they would make an exception for this foreigner. I only wanted to spend a short amount of time with them and not disrupt their daily lives or training regimen.

After riding several miles, we turned down a long rode that seemed to go into the jungle. At the end of the road, I noticed a small walled complex with a front gate. We rode in through the gate and the driver dropped me off and left before I had the chance to tell him to wait for me. I was now in the middle of a large boxing camp, with a training session in full swing.

The noise of the motorcycle caught everyone's attention. They all stopped what they were doing and walked over to me. Almost immediately, I was surrounded in a half circle by more than a dozen Thai boxers that varied in age from eight to the early twenties.

I believe I was the first foreigner they had ever seen in person. They looked me up and down and started talking to each other. They seemed amazed I was there and amused by the way I looked. They were smiling, giggling, and touching me because I was so different from them. None of them spoke English and I didn't speak Thai, so it was both an uncomfortable and an exciting experience.

After a few minutes, one of the boys went to get the head trainer, who was resting in his room. He came out and started speaking to me but soon realized I had no idea what he was saying. But I had my camera in my hand and he assumed I was a tourist that wanted to take some pictures.

He motioned that it would be okay to do so. I was happy to do some shooting, but I really wanted to train with them too. I photographed the rest of their workout, then the boys got cleaned up and ready for dinner.

They swept out the training area and carried in tables that stood only about a foot off the ground. Then they brought out dishes of food and a big pot of rice that were prepared by the camp cook. They all lined up with plates in their hands and scooped out a slab of rice, then sat down.

One of the boxers handed me a plate with rice and motioned for me to sit next to him to eat. There were three main dishes on the table. They were made up of pork, fish, and beef. The food was good and very healthy and there were no soft drinks, only water. Although the fighters eat well, they are on a strict diet so they can keep their weight under control and have enough energy to go through hours of rigorous training every day.

After dinner, the boys cleaned the area, washed the dishes, then went into their living quarters to relax. It was too late in the evening for me to go back to town and find a hotel so they gave me my own spot on the floor with a pillow and a mat to sleep on. The same boy that served me dinner laid my mat next to his and helped me get settled. His name was Leung, and we became friends during my stay. These people had only known me for a few hours, but they took me into their home, fed me, and gave me a place to stay for the night.

At 6 a.m., one of the trainers came in the dormitory and woke everyone for the morning run. The guys reluctantly got up, dressed, and gathered by the front gate. Every training session starts with a group run, and a trainer follows behind on a motorcycle to make sure they all finish without getting sick or passing out. Every fighter made it through the run without a problem.

It's hard for me to imagine that kids as young as ten can be in such great physical condition. He motioned for me to get on the back of his bike so I could take pictures of them running. It was a great opportunity for me to get a shot of all of the fighters together. I wanted to join them, but I decided not to ask so soon. I wanted to give them a chance to get to know me a little; I wasn't sure if they would allow me to train.

During the run, we passed by a few farm houses, Buddhist shrines, and caverns. There were little monkeys running around on the road and climbing the trees, making noises at us as we passed by. Monkeys are as common in Thailand as cats and dogs, but to me it was like being in a zoo. The run went on for about five miles in the intense tropical heat, but none of the boys seemed to be affected by it. Soon we were back at the camp and ready to start the rest of the workout.

The boys started jumping rope while the trainers looked on. I sat down next to Tewa and the assistant trainer, Somchit. Tewa pointed at each of the fighters, telling me their names. I tried to remember as many as I could, but only a few stuck in my head. Thai names are very long, but most Thai people also use short nicknames.

Morning: The First Training Session

While the boxers were preparing for the rest of the training session, Somchit told Leung to wrap my hands. Another boy found me a pair of boxing gloves. They thought I was only there to take pictures and had no experience in Muay Thai. They wanted to show me how hard their training is, and in a friendly way, poke fun at me for not being able to fight.

15

Somchit then led me into one of the boxing rings for some drills. When a trainer works with you in the boxing ring he holds two thick heavy pads called Thai pads in English. You follow him around the ring throwing kicks and punches at the pads while he throws kicks back at you. This allows you to work on your offensive and defensive skills at the same time. And it also gives the trainer the opportunity to teach you new things as well as push you to your endurance limits for three or four rounds.

Before my trip, I had been training consistently for two months to make sure I was in good shape. But the heat and humidity in Thailand really affected my endurance, and the fewer punches and kicks I threw the more he hit me. He was testing to see how much heart I had. They won't respect you if you act like you want to quit so you have to keep going, even if it means taking a beating. The pain and bruises go away, but their opinion of you doesn't change so easily. I wanted to earn Somchai's respect so he would let me keep training with them, so I pushed myself as hard as I could.

All the fighters stopped what they were doing to watch me. I threw my first kick and it smacked hard against the pads. They all looked very surprised and continued to watch me for a few minutes. I really wanted to show them what I had, so I kicked and punched as hard as I could. Being much bigger than any of the boxers, I had more power than most of the boys. But my skills paled in comparison, which I would find out soon enough.

After I suffered through the one-on-one drills with the trainer I found a heavy bag to punch and kick. I was already tired from the torture I endured in the ring, so I could only go through the motions for the rest of the day until the session ended. I was amazed at the physical conditioning that Thai boxers have: they run for miles, then go through another two or three hours of training, twice a day.

The morning workout ended about 9 a.m. then we got ready for break-fast. In Thailand, like many other Asian countries, there is no real breakfast food. They basically eat the same things for every meal. The food was very good, but it was hard for me to eat fish, pork, and rice so early in the morning.

After breakfast, some of the boys went to school while the others laid around. The Phetburi Muay Thai Camp is several miles away from the city, so the guys hang out around the camp most of the time and sleep, read magazines, watch television, or play pool on the table that graced the center of their training area. The camp did have a nice little soccer field though, and a few of the boys started kicking the ball around, so I played with them for awhile to pass the time. I was having fun being around them even though I couldn't speak their language.

After the soccer game, Leung took me into the city on the back of his motorcycle. We rode to the Seven-Eleven and got some snacks. He didn't eat junk food, but I had to have something for myself. Then we went to the local bookstore where he bought a Thai-English dictionary. We were becoming friends and he wanted to communicate with me while I was there.

When we got back to the camp, we sat down and started asking each other questions, using the dictionary. We both had problems pronouncing each other's language, but I eventually learned a few things about his life. He was twenty-four years old and started fighting when he was ten. He told me his family was very poor and that he became a fighter to earn enough money to buy a small piece of land for himself and the girl he planned to marry. He was anxious to quit fighting and move back home to be with her so they could raise a family.

Evening: The Training Continues

The afternoon workout session rolled around and the trainers yelled for the guys to wake up from their naps and get ready to run. It seemed a small challenge to get the boys going, which seemed odd to me because Thai boxers have the reputation as being some of the most aggressive fighters in the world. But most of them are teenagers and they would rather just sit around and watch television or ride into town and hang out with other people their age.

The second training session was harder for me because I was still sore from the morning. I had not trained seriously since I last fought, so my shins were a little bruised and tender from kicking the Thai pads and punching bags. Contrary to what people may believe, the Thai's don't actually do any shin conditioning drills. They kick pads and bags, and spar with each other. And they do injure their legs sometimes; I noticed that most of the boys had bruises on their shins. But the injuries aren't usually serious and eventually heal, their legs getting tougher in the process.

This training session would be a little tougher than the last. I was paired up with a sixteen-year-old boy named Lim. At 140 pounds, he was the closest one to my size. We did some light sparring for three rounds. I had proved I had power, but now it was time to show that I had some skills too. To my amazement, every punch and kick I threw at him was blocked and countered. It was almost as if he knew what I was going to do before I did. I had expected these guys to be exceptional fighters, but I didn't realize how great they really are.

Toward the end of the session, I was put in the ring with a fighter named Silom. We practiced clinching and knee drills. Clinching is done by grabbing your opponent's head from behind with the palms of your boxing gloves, then pulling him around to throw off his balance. Once you have control of him, you pull him into your knee as you strike him. It is probably the most effective technique in any fighting style because of the damage a knee can cause. Although I outweighed Silom by almost fifty pounds, he pulled me around and kneed me at will. Strength is important, but he knew how to use every pound of his weight to his advantage, so I was being thrown around by a much smaller man. The fighters never go all-out when sparring with each other because they fight so often and need to stay healthy. So, Silom never tried to hurt, but I did catch a few knees in my body. It is actually good conditioning for a real fight.

My first full day of training had ended and we were all hanging out in the room when one of the camp managers came in. He noticed me sitting there and asked about me. The boys told him why I was there and he gave one of them some money, then the boy left. He came back about fifteen minutes later with food he bought at the Seven-Eleven. I guess the manager thought I might miss eating American food, so he asked the kid to buy me a hamburger, hot dog, some doughnuts, and a Coke. I thanked him for his gesture, but I had just eaten dinner.

The manager soon left and I had all the food on the floor in front of me. I saw the boys staring at it, so I pushed it towards them. About five of them dove on it, grabbing what they could and taking off out the door while the other boys chased them. The only thing left were the wrappers floating in the air. They eat well, but the chance to eat American food doesn't come very often so it was a nice treat for them.

The boys continued to make conversation with me when we weren't training. I was trying to learn as much about them as I could. One boy in particular had a very interesting story. He was Cambodian and his parents wanted him to become a fighter. Leung told me that when his parents brought him to the camp he was crying and screaming to go home with them. He told me the boy wouldn't quit crying for days, then finally Tewa had to spank him to keep him quiet.

The Cambodian boy, Niran, smiled from embarrassment when he heard the story. He was fully adjusted to living at the camp now, and the Thai's accepted him as one of their own. He seemed somewhat happy, but a little sad too. I had a feeling that he still missed his family very much.

By the time I had found the Muay Thai camp in Phetburi I could only stay a week before I had to go back home. I continued to train with the fighters, but on a limited basis. My main objective of the trip was to shoot the documentary. A lot is known about the sport of Muay Thai because of its growing popularity, but little is known about the fighters' lives. They represent a fascinating part of Thai culture and I wanted to tell their story.

During the week I spent at the camp, I learned a lot about the boxers and about Thai culture in general. I also learned even more about Muay Thai, although I didn't have enough time to better my skills. But I was there for the experience, and it was a great experience. I was a little sad to leave because I made a few new friends and felt like I was becoming a part of their family. I said my goodbyes and headed back to Bangkok, where one of the boys, Nam Suek, was fighting at Lumphini Stadium the next day.

Bangkok: Fight Night at Lumphini Stadium

When I arrived at Lumphini, I was immediately approached by a stadium employee who led me to the ticket counter. I purchased a ringside ticket for 1,000 *baht*, which is about $25.00 US. They give you a fight program of the evening's event, which is nothing more than a piece of paper that's been photocopied. With the program in hand, I sat down and waited until it was time to go inside.

21

The fights start about 6:30 p.m., so they let people enter the arena about 6 p.m. Walking down the corridor, I noticed the trophy case off to one side. It had boxing gloves, Thai boxing shorts, a headband (*mongkon*), and a title belt, along with a few other things. This showcase is an impressive way of letting you know where you are!

When you walk into the arena, the first thing you notice is how small it is. I doubt it seats more than a few thousand people. There is also no air conditioning, but there are plenty of ceiling fans. Since the fights start in the evening, it is actually very comfortable. The absence of modern comforts creates the perfect ambiance fitting for a Muay Thai stadium.

Ringside ticket holders are seated by a stadium representative, and I was lucky to get a front row seat. The first few fights of the evening are preliminary bouts with young boys fighting, who are normally about ten years old. Kids that age have little experience or skill, but they are still fun to watch and seem to get as much response from the crowd as the older fighters.

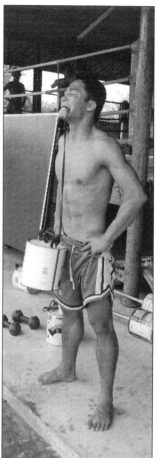

When the fighters enter the arena they walk from the dressing rooms to the ring, passing right in front of you. They kneel and say a prayer before climbing the steps to enter the ring. Then they go through their *wai kru* and *ram muay* to pay homage to their trainers and boxing camp. The wai kru is when the fighters walk to each corner of the ring, saying prayers at each ring post. The ram muay is the actual ceremonial dance.

At the beginning of the event, the band starts playing the traditional music (*wong pee glong*), which lasts throughout the event. When I first started watching Muay Thai fights, I had a difficult time listening to it, but I've grown accustomed to it.

After watching two great fights, Tewa approached me. The boys from the camp had just arrived at the stadium and he had promised to take me into the locker room to watch the fighters get ready. It was a great opportunity for me because they don't normally allow people in there taking pictures.

At Lumphini Stadium, there are no real locker rooms. There is an area behind the concession stand where the fighters are prepared for their bouts. Fans that try to take pictures are quickly led away, but Tewa had arranged for me to be there. It is, however, permissible to pose for pictures with the fighters after they fight.

After Nam Suek had his hands wrapped, he got a massage to loosen him up. After they put his gloves on him, Tewa placed the mongkon on his head and said a prayer. Then it was time to walk to the ring. I saw the nervous look in Nam Suek's eyes, but I noticed his opponent looked very calm and confident.

I walked with them to the ring and stood by the ring apron taking pictures. It was the best seat in the house. The fight lasted into the fifth and final round, then Nam Suek was knocked out by an elbow to his head. It happened so fast, I could barely see what happened. Our fighter was on the canvas a second later and couldn't get up. A stretcher was called and he was carried from the ring.

I felt really bad about what happened. It was hard watching someone I knew get knocked out so violently. He had a large cut above his eye from the strike, but after a few minutes he was okay. That made me think about whether or not this should have happened. A lot of these boys are pushed into becoming fighters for financial or cultural reasons and may not actually want to be doing it. But, it is important to preserve such an important part of Thai culture and it also serves as a rite of passage for young Thai men.

The night I spent watching the fights at Lumphini Stadium was an incredible experience. Every one of the fights were full of action, and half of them ended in knockouts. The main event was a championship fight, in which the champion won. Many fans followed the champion into the back room so they could get their pictures taken with him. Thai boxers are quite different than most professional athletes from other countries in that they are very humble and love to spend time with their fans.

Within a few days after the fights, I was on a plane back home. The flight to Kentucky lasted almost twenty hours, and during the entire time all I could think about was the experiences I had in Thailand. I enjoyed living at the Muay Thai camp, watching the fights, visiting the temples, and meeting new people. There is still so much of the country I didn't have the chance to see. I am already planning my next visit.

chapter 3

Than Quyen:
An Introduction to Spirit Forms
of That Son Vietnamese Martial Arts

by Jason Hoai Tran, B.A.

*All photos of Jason Tran by Maria
Nguyen Thi Ngoc Dung and Elliott Back.*

Introduction

It is common in East Asian martial arts to practice imitation styles (*xing xiang quan*) inspired by the movements and characteristics of animals and spirits. In modern Chinese wushu, such imitation styles include Tiger Style, Praying Mantis, Eagle Claw, Monkey Fist, Snake, and Drunken Fist. Chinese styles based on the powers of spirit deities are also to be found, such as the 18 Shaolin Arhats, Buddha Palm, Bodhidharma Cane, and Monkey King Staff (Liang, 2001: 4). The inspiration and flavor of imitation styles is even more vivid in That Son Than Quyen, Vietnamese martial arts that teach spirit (*quyen*) forms such as Black Tortoise, White Tiger, Celestial Dragon, Black Tiger, Vermillion Phoenix, and Invisible Spirit.

This chapter will study the origin and functions of That Son Than Quyen's spirit forms. This will be accomplished by contrasting Than Quyen with northern (Chinese) imitation styles, tracing the development of religion and superstitions in Vietnam, and exploring the impact of geographic and cultural elements of the That Son Mountain region and their influences on Than Quyen. We will discover that just as Vietnamese Buddhism does not resemble its Chinese counterpart, imitation styles of That Son martial arts differ from Chinese styles. These differences include historical origin, religious background, and societal functions of the art and its practitioners. Than Quyen spirit forms emerged in response to the danger and perceived mystery of the Than Son region. In addition, Than Quyen adepts' social roles differed greatly from those of the lands north of Vietnam.

Northern Imitation Style Martial Arts

By "Northern Styles" this author means any style of martial art that claims direct descent from the Shaolin Temple in Henan Province, China. This includes all Chinese arts mentioned above, modern wushu, and southern styles such as Hung Style, Choy Li Fat, Five Ancestors, and Southern Fist (Liang, 2001: 401, 376, 426). Styles descended from the purported Southern Shaolin Temple in Fujian, as are the latter three, will be considered "northern" in this chapter because of their Shaolin origins.

According to Shaolin tradition, the Buddhist monk Bodhidharma entered the Shaolin Temple during the Northern and Southern Dynasties period (6th C.E.) after "facing the wall" in meditation for nine years. Thereafter, Bodhidharma taught his disciples that, "To achieve enlightenment you must quiet the spirit. The body serves as a shell for the spirit; it must be made strong in order to function. If the spirit is not quiet, it cannot recognize enlightenment and become Buddha. If the body is not strong, the blood and qi will be stagnant" (Liang, 1990: 8). This Zen Buddhist teaching instructs the student to discipline both mind and body. This concept is reflected in the Buddhist statement: "In cultivation, one's nature and one's life form a pair" (Lai, 1999: 206). In accordance with this idea, Bodhidharma modified Dr. Hua Tuo's Five Animal's Dance (wuxing xi), a health building exercise that involved the movements of the tiger, deer, bear, monkey, and bird, to create the first Shaolin imitation style, the Five Animals Boxing style (wuxingquan). This new style imitated the motions of the tiger, leopard, crane, snake, and dragon. The Five Animals Style proved quite effective against bandits around Shaolin Temple (Liang, 1990: 9).

From the above we may conclude that imitation styles at Shaolin Temple developed as a method of defense and more importantly self-cultivation.

Because he believed in both physical and mental training, Bodhidharma was versed in both Zen and *qigong*/yoga. The relationship between his Five Animals Style and self-cultivation are as follows (Qin, 2002):

1) Tiger trains the bones (*gu*)
2) Leopard trains strength (*li*)
3) Crane trains the libido (*jing*)
4) Snake trains vital energy (*qi*)
5) Dragon trains the spirit (*shen*).

The first two animals train the external body while the latter three cultivate internal power (*neigong*). These five are elements of "life" in "one's nature and life form a pair," and thus prerequisite to enlightenment in Bodhidharma's teaching.

 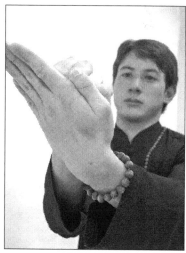

Left: Ready posture. Right: Hammer strike.

Imitation Styles vs. Spirit Forms: The Martial Arts of That Son

For us to appreciate the cultural richness and historic depth embodied in Than Quyen practice, we must contrast this Vietnamese martial art against northern styles. Here I have chosen to label northern animal martial arts "imitation styles" and That Son animal styles "spirit forms." These definitions are intended to illustrate the differences in function and origin of the two. Northern imitation forms were created for self-cultivation and defense. The That Son style, however, was born out of superstition and a perceived need to combat the strange and mysterious.

With these definitions in mind, this chapter now turns to the religious, cultural, and social background of the northern and That Son arts. We will find that the discrepancies between the two can be attributed to differences in geography and environment from which the two emerged.

In the north—despite constant vicissitudes and three periods of persecution (*sanwu yizong*) under the reigns of Emperor Tai Wu (r. 424-452 C.E.) of the Wei Dynasty, Emperor Wu (r. 561-578 C.E.) of the Northern Zhou, and Emperor Wu Zong (r. 841-847 C.E.) of the Tang Dynasty—the Shaolin Temple has more or less maintained itself since Bodhidharma (Lai, 1999: 239). Buddhist (of which Zen is a branch) and Daoist sects were relatively well organized; self-sustained; had their own laws, rituals, and formal initiation ceremonies; and at times enjoyed royal patronage (Lai, 1999: 239; Wang, 2000: 25). Consequently, the northern styles were able to sustain continuous lineages and loyalty to the Shaolin Temple and her related sects on a real or at least imaginary level. As a result, the Shaolin Temple came to be regarded not only as the birthplace of northern martial arts, but also as a place of sanctity, sanctuary, and ferment for martial arts and Buddhist thought. Therefore, a sense of heritage and orthodoxy (*zheng zong*) are paramount in northern styles.

The situation in Vietnam is much different. The three religious schools (*san jiao*: Confucianism, Buddhism, Daoism) were never systematized and organized in Vietnam to the extent that they were in the north. A Buddhist-official class succeeded in creating an educated elite in the south. However, their attempts to create an orthodoxy fell short and, instead, they merely created a thin external shell of educated Buddhist rhetoric that became saturated with mysticism and magic due to the pressures of the masses and their obsessions with the supernatural. Moreover, whereas the Shaolin Temple was a place of sanctity, the jungle depths of That Son were a realm of danger, mystery, and awe. Moreover, the people of That Son were not ethnic Vietnamese, but rather people the Vietnamese regarded as strange and bizarre forest peoples. As a result, in contrast to the north, That Son martial arts evolved not only in response to the human battlefield, but also to combat the invisible powers of the unknown and supernatural.

Buddhist Sorcery of the Southern Vietnamese

Buddhism in Vietnam can be traced as early as the late 6th century with the pilgrimage of Vinitaruci (*Ty Ni Da Luu Chi*) from India to China and finally Vietnam. He is purported to have founded the first Buddhist school in Vietnam. However, there is convincing evidence that the monk never reached Vietnam and that his biography in the *Thien Uyen Tap Anh* (*A*

28

Collection of Outstanding Figures of the Zen Community) was reconstructed by its compiler in an attempt to create the "orthodox shell" described above (Nguyen, 1997: 37). Its orthodoxy is largely suspect. Later, Buddhism enjoyed its greatest popularity under the Ly Dynasty (1010-1225). The Ly Dynasty was founded by a Buddhist martial artist, Ly Cong Uan (reigned as Ly Thai To, 1010-1028), who had been raised and trained at Co Phap Buddhist Temple (Nguyen, 1996: 111). However, it would be inaccurate to label the Ly Dynasty as simply Buddhist. Instead, perhaps the term "Vietnamese spiritualism" would be more precise. The Vietnamese had just rid themselves of one thousand years of northern, Tang Chinese, occupation. Nevertheless, they did not reject Chinese culture and religion. The forms these religions assumed, however, varied greatly from the north, in a period Keith Taylor describes as, "varied, experimental, and nonexclusive" and that the Vietnamese were "too absorbed by the excitement of discovering and constructing their own culture to erect barriers against any particular influence. Buddhist monks, [D]aoist priests, and classical literati all had positive contributions to make" (Taylor, 1986: 149). Ly Dynasty Vietnamese were searching for their identity, their "spirit."

This "Vietnamese spiritualism" reached peak fever when King Ly Nhan Ton (r. 1072-1127) failed to produce an heir. As a result, anyone claiming spiritual potency immediately won favor with the king, as the king hoped that their magic would grant him a son. This search for spiritual adepts went on irrespective of religious affiliation. All sects, whether Buddhist, Daoist, or pure shamanistic, were involved. In fact, each group need only share one commonality, spiritual power. There is a famous story in which a Daoist, Thong Huyen, and a Buddhist monk, Giac Hai, combined their Daoist magic and Buddhist sorcery to slay two toad-like demons that attacked the palace. Afterward, Ly Nhan Ton praised them in poetic verse (Le, 1999: 35).

> Giac Hai's mind is truly as vast as the sea.
> Thong Huyen is indeed mysterious.
> Their powers divine and spirits unyielding,
> True to their names, one a Buddha, one an immortal.

Giac Hai is also known for a pilgrimage he took to India with fellow Buddhist sorcerers Dao Hanh and Minh Khong. The three arrived at their destination through the help of a ferryman-spirit and returned using the magic they acquired in India. Of the three, Dao Hanh became the most powerful. To repay an old debt to Marquis Sung Hien and to resolve Ly Nhan Ton's dilemma, Dao Hanh used his magic to propel his spirit embryo into the womb of the marquis' wife. After he passed away, Dao Hanh reincarnated as the marquis' son, whom King Ly Nhan Ton adopted, and later ascended to the throne as King Ly Than Ton (r. 1128-1138).

From this story we can conclude that Vietnamese Buddhists were more concerned with spiritual potency than piety. The Vietnamese obsession with the divine and the weird would continue into the 18th century, when the confusion of the three religions continued to be obscured by the cloak of sorcery. Buddhist sorcerers utilized their Zen "orthodox shell," filling it with Tantric mystic syllables (*dharanis*), Buddhist hand gestures (*mudra*) and mystic chants (*mantra*), and Daoist qigong and magic charms.

A-1-8 Mudras: Mudras or Tantric hand gestures are used in That Son martial arts to invoke spirits, meditate, and regulate qi flow. Each mudra is associated with a Chinese character, and a meditative "mood" or spirit. They are often combined with pronouncing mystic syllables and singing Buddhist chants.

In 1750, Father Adriano Di St. Thecla, a missionary in northern Vietnam, composed the *Opusculum* (*A Small Treatise on the Sects Among the Chinese and Tonkinese*). Di St. Thecla recorded many of the spiritual practices of 18th century northern Vietnamese. For instance, he noted that each city had its own Genie Protector (*thanh hoang*) and that people were forced to pledge allegiance to their lord in the presence of gods at a Hoi Minh festival. In addition, he observed the overlapping roles of exorcism held by Daoist and Buddhist. Di St. Thecla dubbed Daoism the "Magicians' Sect" and Buddhism the "Worshippers' Sect." In his chapter on "Magicians," he writes that Daoist "masters of sorcery" (*thay phu thuy*, "masters of charm water") used magic to cure sickness by exorcising twenty-four evil spirits, five of whom were most feared. They also invoked the spirit of the Black Tigress (Di St. Thecla, 2003: 165). In Di St. Thecla's chapter on "Worshipers," he observes that Buddhist, too, invoked spirits in their ceremonies and exorcisms. They included such spirits as the White King, Black King, and Red King (Di St. Thecla, 2003: 213). These kings refer to spirits of Daoist astrology and correspond to the cardinal directions. They are the Black Tiger, White Tiger, Black Tortoise, and Vermillion Phoenix, names of That Son spirit forms, mentioned in the opening paragraph of this research.

Buddhist Warriors and Sorcerers of the Seven Mountains

The *That Son* (lit. "Seven Mountains") in Chau Doc Province of southern Vietnam were not inhabited by ethnic Vietnamese until 1759, nine years after Father Di St. Thecla completed the *Oposculum* (Nguyen, 1972: 22). Thus, the Vietnamese beliefs in the supernatural that he described were magnified by the new dangerous, uncultivated, land they encountered and the strange forest people who dwelled there. These Vietnamese were frontiersmen in a bizarre, unfamiliar, land. One can only imagine the reactions of so superstitious a people to such an adventure into the mysterious.

In the new southern lands, the Vietnamese continued to rely on Buddhist sorcery and magic to protect them as they had done in the past. This is the reason That Son spirit forms evolved to include so many spirit guardian and forest animal spirit forms. Unlike the north, it was not good enough for a martial monk/sorcerer to possess merely self-defense and combat skills. Any soldier could do that! The martial monk needed to convince his adversary that his skills were inspired by the divine, that he was protected by god, or even that he was possessed. More importantly, he needed to demonstrate to common folk that he had supernatural power. What better way than through spirit forms! The effect of such martial performances in "God of the Northern Skies Black Tortoise King" or "White Tiger Forest Guardian" on the anxious minds of Vietnamese frontiersmen would have been no less than awesome. It was not fighting ability that determined the power of the That Son martial artist, but rather his spiritual charisma and its expression through his art.

In addition, Buddhists and mystics amplified the majesty of That Son through beliefs in *fengshui*. They determined that the five mountains and seven peaks of That Son lie on a *fengshui* "Dragon Channel" between the "Golden Fortress Channel" of the Mekong River and the Chau Doc Mountains. These channels are thought to carry the energy of the Himalayas, where Sakyamuni was enlightened, and focus it at That Son. It is further believed that That Son is perfectly situated to harness the energies of the "Central Water Channel" at Ha Tien, the "Mystic Gate Channel" at Tay Ninh, the "On the Verge of Mystery Channel" at Ca Mau, the "Emerald Jade Channe" at Ky Van, and the "Peaceful South Channel" at Con Non (Nguyen, 1972: 47). It is worth noting that two of these fengshui channels, "Mystic Gate" and "On the Verge of Mystery," closely match the names of That Son spirit forms.

B-1-5 Tiger Style: One who assumes the tiger spirit is fierce. The muscles are tensed like a tiger ready to pounce, which stores energy like a bow string about to release an arrow. Tigers on Mt. Nui Cam (The Forbidden Mountain) are said to be Buddhist protector spirits.

C-1-7 Dragon Style: This spirit is like a dragon plunging into the sea. The stances are extremely low with circular movements that mimic the coiling motion of a dragon in flight. Dragons are reputed to possess powers of transformation.

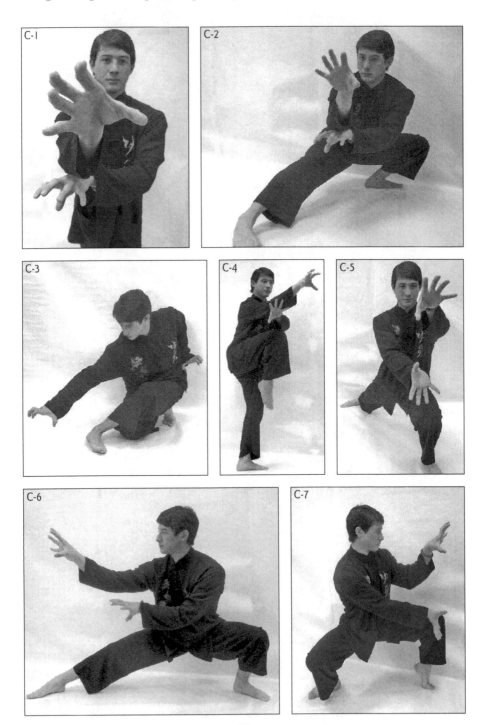

D-1-5 Snake Style: This is the softest of the seven spirits. The movements yield to the opponent's force, entangles him, and uses venomous pressure point strikes that require a minimum of force. Snake spirits were said to be seductive forest demons that have the ability to assume other forms.

E-1-4 Crane Style: The crane spirit embodies harmony and peace of mind. Cranes are spirits of longevity and immortality in Vietnamese lore.

F-1-3 Monkey Style: Agility is the monkey spirit's greatest attribute and uses speed to overcome an opponent of superior size and strength. The monkey represents wisdom.

G-1-3 Hawk Style: The hawk spirit is noble and brave. Its movements are swift with a penetrating, cutting, power.

H-1-6 Phoenix Style: The phoenix is to soar, embodying freedom of movement. Towering above the earth, broad vision is its virtue. The phoenix is a Yin spirit with soft, natural, movements.

I-1-7 Weapons: Halberd and sword.

The Vernerable Buddha Master and His Twelve Disciples

Perhaps the greatest Buddhist master of That Son was Doan Minh Huyen (1807-1856), whom the people of Chau Doc know only as *Phat Thay* ("Buddha Master") (Nguyen, 1971: 77). Phat Thay left his home village of Tong Son in his youth. Where he went no one knows, but he returned in 1849 a powerful Buddhist sorcerer. He first exercised his acquired powers as he returned to his home village. When he got to Tong Son, he saw the entire village gathered around and trying to pull an enormous log from the river, which was a vital transportation route. After several hours, the villagers were still unable to remove the log. Finally, Phat Thay instructed them to tie a rope around the log. He then used a hand mudra and recited a mantra while they pulled. The log was pulled effortlessly to shore. Before the villagers could appreciate the feat that had been performed, Phat Thay already vanished from the scene (Nguyen, 1972: 62).

There are no records of Phat Thay ever using martial arts. However, many of his famous twelve disciples were skilled warriors. Such martial arts masters include Cui Da and Potato Seller Vai. There is also a story of Dinh and his battles against a Forest Snake Demon. Perhaps Phat Thay's most celebrated disciple was Venerable Duc Co Quan (?-1873), who took to arms and apparently died fighting French imperialists. His son, Ong Hai Van Nhu, also possessed great martial abilities, which he used to fight and escape his enemies after being surrounded. Lost and the sole survivor of the battle, he was rescued by a forest tiger spirit that guided him to safety (Nguyen, 1972: 167). A poem of his father, Duc Co Quan, is still remembered by local Vietnamese (Nguyen, 1972: 118):

> Rather than suffer defeat, I shall fight in due repose,
> And drag out the heads of all tyrants who oppose our lord and ministers.
> Let Heaven and Earth determine my fate,
> And compel me to repay my debts of righteousness and grace in full!
> – author's translation

From Duc Co Quan's poem we can infer that Phat Thay's teachings emphasized helping others and alleviating people's suffering. The praise of common people added a didactic element to Phat Thay's already potent image.

Little can be determined about Phat Thay's philosophy. We do know, however, that he was very esoteric. In fact, his brand of spiritual practice differed greatly from his fellow Buddhists in the Zen Lam Te School (Chin. *Linji*; Jap. *Renzai*), already established at That Son before his arrival. Unlike

39

the Lam Te Buddhists, Phat Thay did not rely on sutra study or Buddhist idolatry. He did, however, instruct the patients he cured to chant praise to the Bodhisattva Avalokitesvara (*Quan The Am, Niem Phat*). He also adhered to the Buddhist three points of study (*tam hoc*): 1) discipline, 2) Zen quietude, and 3) wisdom (Nguyen, 1971: 62). In this respect, Phat Thay's teaching resembled the Zen of northern China. His disciple Master Bon also reflected similar Zen beliefs in this poem:

> The meditation chamber, half aglow, half dim, leading to intrigue,
> But this eternal heart can never be deceived.
> Do not regard the heavens as high, nor Gods and Saints afar.
> You must first respect and understand your own person.
> As the Bodhi chants and chants forever without suffering,
> Achieves the dharma, completes life, and in happiness liberates all beings.
> Escape the dust of illusion, sprinkling sweet dew,
> In perfect wisdom, guard the mind's mysteries.
> – author's translation

Nevertheless, Phat Thay transmitted a unique Buddhist teaching, which he summarized with the "four debts of kindnesses to be treasured and repaid" (*tu an*). They are:

1. Debt to the ancestors and one's parents.
2. Debt to one's country.
3. Debt to the three Buddhist Treasures—the three refuges or vows: refuge in the Buddha, in the Dharma, and in monkhood (*sangha*).
4. Debt to humanity.

From this we may conclude that Phat Thay's teachings revolved not only around personal salvation but also that the Buddhism of That Son was deeply concerned with humanity and performing good deeds. Though Phat Thay himself was obscure and often lived in seclusion "outside the world," the spiritual philosophy and martial arts he entrusted to his disciples served to "enter the world" and end the sufferings of the dangerous yet mystical world that was That Son.

• • •

Here we conclude this chapter with the following poem, the mysteries of That Son as described by Venerable Duc Huynh Giao Chu, founder of Vietnamese Hoa Hao Buddhism.

Grand peaks emerge from That Son,
Just look at them and you shall know their marvels!
As the vermillion peaks of the seven mountains reveal themselves,
You would think that the aged could be restored to youth!
Among the seven mountains marvelous treasures abound,
Endeavor to cultivate the mind and perfect your nature
– watch over this world.
Atop the five peaks dwell brilliant dragons and phoenixes.
And beyond the seven mountains exist yet greater wonders!
If only the world would know it in time and learn…
To see the mysterious jewel of the five peaks.
In the grand peaks of Forbidden Mountain are
revealed tomorrow and yesterday.
Awakened, the masses will finally see expressed,
The forests of trees and stone seen today,
Are the soul of the five mountains and their towering forms.[1]

> – author's translation

Note

[1] The That Son Than Quyen spirit forms are modeled after the region from which they emerged. In addition to its relation to astrology and *fengshui*, That Son Than Quyen includes spirits forms that reflect the region's physical geography. These are the Five Gates and Seven Spirits (*Ngu Mon That Linh*). Just as there are discrepancies in the Five Peaks and Seven Mountains, it is also difficult to determine exactly which spirits belong to the That Linh, as many more than seven spirit forms are practiced in That Son Than Quyen. According to the *Classic of That Son Than Quyen*, the five gates refer to the five elements: wood, fire, earth, metal, and water; while the seven spirits are tiger, crane, hawk, snake, monkey, phoenix, and dragon.

Bibliography

Di St. Thecla, A. (2002). *Opusculum de sectis apud Sinenses et Tunkinenses: A small treatise on the sects among the Chinese and Tonkinese.* (Olga Dror, Trans.). Ithaca, NY: Southeast Asia Program Publications.

Lai, Y. H. (1999). *Theorizing Chinese Buddhist culture*. Beijing: China Youth Publishing House. In Chinese.

Le, M. T. (1999). *Research into the Thien Uyen Tap Anh*. Ho Chi Minh City: Ho Chi Minh Publishing House. In Vietnamese.

Liang, B. (1990). *True records of Shaolin Temple's internal and external martial arts*. Beijing: Beijing Physical Education University Press.

Liang, S., and Wen, C. W. (2001). *Kung fu elements*. East Providence, RI: Way of the Dragon Publishing.

Ly, T. X. (1961). *Le Huu Mu* [A collection of Vietnamese spirit tales]. (Le Huu Muc, Trans.). Saigon: Khai Tri Publishing House.

Nguyen, C. T. (1997). *Zen in medieval Vietnam: A study and translation of the Thien Uyen Tap Anh*. Honolulu, HI: University of Hawaii Press.

Nguyen, V. H. (1971). *Half a month in the That Son region*. Saigon: Huong Sen Xuat Ban.

Nguyen, V. H., and Dat, S. (1972). *That Son the mysterious*. Tu Tam: Nha Xuat Ban Tu Tam.

Nguyen, V. T. (1996). *Buddhist thought in Ly Dynasty culture*. Toronto: Modern Press.

Qin, Q. (2002, Spring). Personal interview during martial arts instruction, Beijing.

Taylor, K. (1986). Authority and Legitimacy in 11th Century Vietnam. In David Marr and A.C. Milner (Eds.), *Southeast Asia in the 9th to 14th centuries*. Singapore: Institute of Southeast Asian Studies.

Tran, J. (2004, January 16). Classic of seven mountain spirits martial arts. Available online: http://www.rso.cornell.edu/sevenspirits/articles.php.

Wang, G. (2000). *A text on Daoist intellectual thought*. Beijing: Religion Publishing House. In Chinese.

chapter 4

Leth Wei & Khun Khmer Boran:
Fighting Arts of Burma and Cambodia

by Scott Mallon

Cambodian boxing camp group photo.
All photos courtesy of Scott Mallon.

Introduction

Slightly less than eleven years ago, I began traveling to Thailand to train in Muay Thai, the national sport of the country. Two years and numerous trips later, I decided to take a chance and move to the country on a one year trial basis. I sold my business and most of my worldly possessions and with two suitcases in hand, hopped on a plane bound for Thailand. The next year was spent roaming the country, learning the language and of course, training in Thai boxing. One year stretched into two years, then three and, before I knew it, I was calling Thailand my home.

Once you get past being a tourist, life in Thailand is much like life anywhere. One of the main reasons I continued to live here though is that it offers the opportunity to journey throughout Southeast Asia easily and affordably. Never happy sitting behind a desk, this was important to me. As a foreigner residing in Thailand, it's necessary that I go out of the country every three months and renew my visa. Some abhor this requirement and view it as a major inconvenience; I look at it as a vacation and an opportunity to travel to new and exciting places.

43

Kampucheau: The Land of Cambodian Kickboxing

One of my excursions to neighboring Kampucheau (Cambodia) eventually led to my discovery of Cambodian kickboxing or *Khun Khmer Boran*. Some of the hotel staff where I was staying informed me of a boxing event taking place and I then quickly made my way to the dilapidated airplane hanger where the event was being held. The main event pit Cambodian champion Ae Pho Thoung against Sudanese fighter Boreykila Faisan Nakaria. The fight was sensational throughout and in round five Ae Pho Thoung, who was ahead in the fight, was unexpectedly and violently knocked out by a devastating ax kick. Seeing their champion defeated, the Cambodian audience, enraged, began launching their steel chairs into the ring. A mass of onlookers rushed to the only two exits in the building, creating a bottleneck of human flesh. The result was an abundance of battered and bruised fans. In order to avoid being crushed, I was forced to climb over a ten foot chain link fence and on to the top of a truck that was serving as a refreshment stand. The incident was frightening and a disaster was only narrowly averted. My first experience as a Cambodian kickboxing fan was nearly my last.

Kampucheau or Cambodia, as it is most commonly known, is a poor, oft-forgotten country, mainly known to the world as the land of the Angkor Wat, genocide, the Khmer Rouge and a place where pedophiles prowl for children virtually unimpeded. Backpackers come in droves for the cheap hotels, the cheap lifestyle and sightseeing. Thai expatriates come to renew their visas and date Khmer and Vietnamese women. The mainstream martial arts community often overlooks this impoverished, far-away country and focuses more on its wealthier neighbor, Thailand.

The people of Cambodia are surprisingly open and friendly, considering all the previous generation has been through. Cambodia is the sort of place that slowly takes hold of you and once it hooks you, it never lets go. It's an odd place, but there's a sliver of normalcy squeezed in between what only can be described as controlled chaos and utter mayhem. In the last few years, due largely to an assortment of grants and loans from various countries, the country has begun showing signs of progress. The main streets have had much of the garbage removed, casinos are springing up, and Western Union has finally made it possible for tourists to obtain any necessary replenishment of funds.

The Cambodian Style of Kickboxing: Khun Khmer Boran

The three best known and widely practiced martial arts in Cambodia are Chinese wushu, taekwondo and traditional Khmer boxing. Traditional Khmer boxing is the most popular of these and is known by a variety of names such as Khun Khmer Boran, Sovanna Phum (Golden Village Boxing), Badai

Serei, or simply kickboxing. Even the most experienced martial artists may not have heard of these. Like many of Southeast Asia's kickboxing styles, Cambodian kickboxing is virtually identical to Muay Thai.

During the reign of the Khmer Rouge (1975-1999), around the time Thai boxing was just becoming recognized worldwide, Khun Khmer Boran was banned from being practiced and slowly began its slide into oblivion. The martial arts scene in Cambodia is now reemerging though, and is finally returning to its pre-Khmer Rouge state. The comeback has begun.

There is a profusion of gyms scattered throughout the country with the best fighters coming from the tiny little border town of Koh Kong. The Thais and Cambodians often make their way across the border to fight each other and it is for this reason that the fighters of Koh Kong tend to be superior to those from elsewhere. Phnom Penh tends to stage the larger fight cards though as this is where the sponsors are based. Most gyms are poorly equipped by any standard and it's amazing that with little more than a pair or two of kicking pads and one or two heavy bags fighters can develop any skill at all. Gyms sometimes use old canvas sacks or rice bags for their heavy bag and training in Khmer kickboxing is as low-tech as it can get. The quality of the fighters is sometimes lacking but the fights are entertaining scraps, at times looking like school yard brawls. Cambodian fighters favor the use of elbows which often makes for stirring bouts. While their skill level is on the rise, they still lag behind the refined technique of the Thais.

Left: Champion Khmer boxer, Ae Pho Thoung, standing left
of the driver who took me to watch a training session.
Right: Old canvas sacks used for heavy bag practice.

The long-time champion of traditional Khmer boxing is 25 year old Ae Pho Thoung. With approximately 175 fights and only 5 losses, he is familiar to most Khmers, liked by many and always the subject of the Khmer boxing fan. He has been champion for three years and now makes movies when he is not fighting. By western standards, however, he leads a frugal existence. No entourage or fancy cars, no big house and most importantly, no big money. He leads a simple life, one that most westerners can not begin to fathom and instead of obtaining wealth, he achieves notoriety.

Khun Khmer Boran

As in Thai kickboxing, Khun Khmer Boran utilizes a variety of punching and kicking techniques, plus the use of knees and elbows.

Khun Khmer Boran
A modern boxing ring. Gloves are used today
for both safety and to help promote the sport.

47

Myanmar: The Land of Burmese Kickboxing

**This is Burma
and it will be quite
unlike any land you
know about.**
– Rudyard Kipling, 1898

One of the world's poorest countries, Myanmar (formerly known as Burma) is relatively unknown to the outside world. Ask a westerner where Myanmar or Burma is on the map and most likely you will get a puzzled response. The country has been under military leadership since 1962 and has been led by the current administration, the State Peace and Development Council (SPDC), since 1988. When the military rule rejected the results of the elections in 1990 and refused to step down, international sanctions were imposed, resulting in global isolation that still exists today.

The iron-fisted Burmese government is known to be heavily involved in the drug trade, mainly opium, methamphetamines and heroin, and those who oppose, question or speak poorly of the government are promptly jailed. Approximately 15,000 students, journalists, doctors, boxers, entertainers and politicians have been imprisoned in the last fifteen years. This is the backdrop in which Burmese boxing is practiced. Burmese boxing was banned from 1886 until 1948 when the nation once again enjoyed its sovereignty. Only recently has the government begun promoting Burmese boxing in hopes of better presenting the sport to the rest of the world and true progress has yet to be made. Certainly though, the political troubles of the country have not helped in any fashion.

The Art of Leth Wei

Burmese boxing or Leth Wei dates back to the Pyu Empire around 800 CE. Rules parallel those of Muay Thai and Cambodian kickboxing, however participants fight without gloves, wrapping their hands in hemp rope or gauze cloth. These wraps provide little in the way of padding and cause frequent cuts and abrasions. Head butts and throws are also allowed. Each fight lasts five three-minute rounds and the contests are often wild and bloody. Victory comes by surrender or knockout, and if both participants are still standing at the end of the bout, it's declared a draw. In some cases, fighters who were knocked out are revived and given the option to fight on, usually until they are knocked out three times. Battling without gloves demands that the boxers be well prepared to absorb repeated blows to the head and a heavy build-up of scar tissue is practically guaranteed.

In the past, bouts were held in sand or dirt pits, however this has increasingly given way to standard boxing rings. In contrast to Khun Khmer Boran and Muay Thai, Leth Wei contests are generally only held during festivals or as a special event and boxers often travel around the country in search of fights. The boxers are to some extent akin to old-time pugilists who fought bare-knuckle in England and America in the 1800s and early 1900s. They fight primarily to survive and feed their families and are willing to fight anyone, anywhere, anytime. There are Leth Wei gyms all over Myanmar. However, unlike in Thailand and even Cambodia, these gyms are not easily found or accessible to foreigners. If you don't know the right people or get lucky, it's just as rare to come across a Leth Wei affair.

In 2001, three American fighters, Doug Evans, Shannon Ritch and Alberto Ramirez went to Yangon, Myanmar, to battle the Burmese. All were summararily knocked out in the first round. Ramirez gave up and both Ritch and Evans were knocked out by knees to the solar plexus. Although there was some controversy in the Evans bout, a rematch never took place and probably never will. There are very few skilled, bare-knuckle fighters in the western hemisphere and even less willing to travel and compete against the Burmese.

Burma is distinctly different from anywhere else I've traveled. The sights, the sounds, the people, the government of course, and nearly everything about the place are unlike what most westerners are accustomed too. On one of my trips I was lucky enough to meet Wan Chai, a former champion and probably the most famed Burmese boxer ever. He is also the fighter who defeated American Doug Evans. Like many Burmese, Thai and Cambodian fighters, Wan Chai has lost track of exactly how many fights he's had but he estimates around one hundred and fifty, the majority of which he has won. Both he and I speak Thai and therefore were able to communicate quite easily. He turned out to be quite down to earth and someone I now consider a friend. When possible, we would go to a teahouse to sit around for a few hours drinking tea (as many Burmese do) and talked about boxing.

Left: A sign in front of Yangon City's Sports Centre.
Right: Shannon Ritch prepares to fight Leth Wei style.
Below: Trainer, Wan Chai, and local guide.

Leth Wei

Along the streets of Yangon City can be found Buddhist temples and boxing arenas featuring Leth Wei. The style has similarities with Thai boxing, but has kept more rooted to the brutal past. Notice the elbow strike to the head in the photograph shown below.

Where Now?

While Thai boxing has literally exploded in popularity across the globe, Khun Khmer Boran and Leth Wei are heading in their own directions. In Cambodia foreigners are now training and fighting regularly and there are between four and six fight cards per week. The Cambodian public is always hungry for a good fight. With the help of two TV stations (Channel 5 and CTN) and sponsors—like M150, Nestle and Caribao Daeng—Cambodian kickboxing is on the mend. The sport has a long way to go, but it has come back a long way already and is gaining momentum.

Both countries have a relatively small pool of fighters compared to Thailand, and it's doubtful this will change in the near future. The reason is simple: money. In Thailand fighters can earn a livable wage and champions can make 200,000 *baht* ($5000 U.S.) or more. Burmese and Cambodian boxers might receive $25 per fight with champions fortunate to receive $500-$1,000. As is the case in many countries, rarely can they make a living exclusively from boxing. The one constant is they always give their all. In contrast to some western fighters, most would rather be knocked out and give a good showing than avoid punishment and give a poor performance.

Burmese currency note of 1,000 kyats, which equals about $180 USD.

Momentum or not, it is difficult for Cambodian fighters to earn a living. The Khmers could almost certainly earn higher purses and gain more recognition were they to unite with the World Muay Thai Council in Thailand, however this is highly unlikely. In their opinion the art of Muay Thai originated in Cambodia and was "stolen" from them by the Thais. They feel it would be beneath them to concede this to the Thais. There are drawings on the Cambodian temple Angkor Wat which perhaps support this notion, however this is and probably always will be a subject of great debate. Regardless of who first discovered the art, the fact is the Thais have marketed and promoted Muay Thai into what it is today—a sport recognized and practiced worldwide and on the verge of becoming an Olympic event. There is a chance the Cambodians may join a U.S. based organization though and this could help their cause.

Over the last few years and possibly thanks to the growing awareness of Muay Thai, Burmese boxing has slowly become more internationally familiar. Fighting with bare-knuckles or wrapped hands will still probably never be accepted outside of Asia. Some observers already view Thai boxing as a brutal sport and perhaps the only way Leth Wei will ever be received as a sport in the western world is if gloves are mandatory and head butts are prohibited. This alters and detracts greatly from the art. Couple this with the oppressive government and I don't see any inroads being made in the near future. At this point, it's too early to tell what the future holds for either art. Cambodians must find a way to compete on a larger scale with their Thai and western counterparts. More importantly, they must get past the feeling that the Thais stole their art. Recently on TV, a weekly boxing show did a short piece about Ae Pho Thoung, the Cambodian champion. Khun Khmer Boran seems to finally be on the verge of breaking into the consciousness of the martial arts public.

Burmese temple complex of white,
green, red, and gold, with marble.

As long as politics are intertwined with Leth Wei, it will always be a challenge to popularize the art. Combine this with the rules currently in use and the challenge is even greater. Outsiders don't want to travel halfway around the world for little to no pay and then have a government use them for their self-serving interests. It seems the only plausible means of Burmese boxing progressing as a sport the martial arts masses can practice is if the government becomes a democratic one. Hopefully this will take place in the near future not only for the good of Burmese boxing but also for the good of those living in Myanmar.

chapter 5

Cultural Myths: Unpacking the Origins of Muay Thai

by Loh Han Loong, B.S.

Photograph © Marcel Braendli / 123RF.com

Muay Thai, otherwise known as the "science of eight limbs," is a fighting system native to Thailand that incorporates the use of hands, elbows, knees, and legs. In recent years Muay Thai has been gaining popularity and renown in the international fighting scene, as even mixed martial artists start to incorporate Muay Thai into their arsenal of lethal techniques. Correspondingly, this has led to increased coverage of Muay Thai in various media. I argue that despite the rapid proliferation of articles, academic or otherwise, that deal with Muay Thai, there are stark similarities in the ways in which Muay Thai has been portrayed. First I will highlight some of the popular depictions of Muay Thai that permeate popular culture and question the veracity of these depictions. Next I will provide some explanations as to why Muay Thai is often presented as such to the man in the street.

The ways in which Muay Thai is framed in popular culture can be categorized as follows: (1) Muay Thai as having its origins in some long-forgotten past, or (2) Muay Thai as being an essential part of Thai culture. However, these two categories are not exclusive, and the boundaries between the two are often blurred. This is exemplified in these narratives about Muay Thai, which draw upon and perpetuate popular understandings of what Muay Thai is:

> Muay Thai is not only one of the most brutal fighting styles in the world, it is a significant part of Thai culture. Its origins go back hundreds of years when the Thai (Siamese) armies used it to defend their borders against foreign invaders. Aside from Buddhism, Muay Thai has linked every class of Thai society together, being practiced by great kings as well as poor farm boys.
>
> —Skaggs, 2003: 49

> Thailand's national sport [Muay Thai] traces its history back to the *Ramayana*, a Hindu story of good vs. evil depicted in many Thai temples. The sport's moves and stances are actually derived from fights detailed in the epic.
>
> —Allan, 2002: 47

These narratives about Muay Thai emphasize its ancient history, and that it is a means by which Thailand maintains its sovereignty. Such an argument is only possible because there is a conflation of the historical developments of Thailand and the history of Muay Thai. This romanticized narrative, which associates Muay Thai with the history of Thailand, translates to Muay Thai's being an inherent part of Thai history, a fundamental part of the culture, and a way by which Thailand defends and expresses herself. In addition, when Skaggs (2003: 49) talks about how "Muay Thai has linked every class of Thai society together, being practiced by great kings as well as poor farm boys," Muay Thai is again explicitly linked to Thai nationalism. There is an attempt to link Muay Thai to Thailand and to the Thai king, who is said to be the symbol of the nation. The implication is that by association to the Thai king, Muay Thai is a highly respected and reputable martial art.

This way in which Muay Thai is constructed is not only prevalent in popular culture, but is also used in the official discourses made by the Thai government. For example, the Muay Thai Institute, an organization specifically endorsed by the Thai government to promote Muay Thai, similarly depicts Muay Thai as follows:

Muaythai [sic] is the cultural heritage descended from the ancestors for centuries. In the past, Thailand had numerous wars with its neighbors. Thai males had to practice Muaythai and other weapons to defend the country. Muaythai has been developed to have its own identity, with graceful but ferocious style. It was practiced for self-defense, health, and profession.

–http://www.muaythai-institute.net/html/history.html

Pagoda on the top of Doi Inthanon, the highest mountain in Thailand. *Photograph by Chatchai Somwat.*

To reiterate my previous argument, the theme of Muay Thai as the mechanism by which to ward off foreign entities is constantly being repeated and emphasized. Muay Thai becomes the means by which Thais define their own sense of identity vis-à-vis foreigners because Muay Thai, as featured in myths and historical tales, has been used by Thais to "defend the country" and "defend their borders against foreign invaders." By positing Muay Thai as the means by which Thais defend their territory, Muay Thai then comes to be a means of defining what is Thailand, and is a way Thais can come to think about Thailand as a nation. In short, such a discourse, perpetuated in popular culture, assumes the following: (1) there is only one form of Muay Thai, (2) Siam and Thailand are synonymous entities given the discourse that Muay Thai has been around for centuries, and (3) Muay Thai "naturally" came into existence to allow Thais to defend themselves historically, without considering who are the people responsible for the creation and perpetuation of this particular discourse.

However, using historical evidence I will be contesting these narratives to demonstrate how they are created by different social actors who have different motives in mind. Historically, there exists not one form of Muay Thai, but many variants, something these narratives have conveniently forgotten to mention. The imagery of war is constantly evoked to show how Muay Thai is a masculine warrior art that has been repeatedly called upon to "defend the country." Not only does this valorize the art of Muay Thai, but individuals learning it can be said to partake and perpetuate the heroic narrative enshrouding previous warriors who took up Muay Thai to defend Thailand. The origins of Muay Thai thus become the history of the Thai nation-state that is constantly perpetuated, even in modern times, as Thais take up Muay Thai for various reasons. In addition, the multifaceted nature of Muay Thai as being a martial art and cultural product that is "graceful and ferocious" is repeatedly highlighted in depictions of Muay Thai in popular culture, once again linking it to Thai identity. I argue, then, that narratives such as Skaggs's, which specifically target martial art aficionados or practitioners, often contain a short introduction of a simplistic and uncritical history of the development of Muay Thai (for examples, see Krauss, Cordoza, and Yingwitayakhun 2006; Delp 2005). These narratives ignore how Muay Thai is a nationalist historiographical project that links Muay Thai to *khwaampenthai* or "Thainess." This nationalist project not only ignores how Siam and Thailand are not synonymous territories (Thongchai, 1994), but, more important, establishes a cultural foundation by which Thai identity can be constructed (Vail, 1998). As such, Muay Thai thus becomes the means by which Thais are able to see themselves as being part of the nation-state of Thailand.

Photograph by Nakit Jaroonsrirak.

Unsurprisingly, then, the origins of Muay Thai are relatively recent. In the past, there was not any unified system of *muay*, defined by Wit (2001:

417) as "boxing, pugilism." Muay Thai can only be said to have developed much later, after the founding of Thailand, during the reigns of King Chulalongkorn and King Vajiravudh (Junlakan and Payukvong, 2001). The creation of what is later known as Muay Thai is attributed to the efforts of King Chulalongkorn, who designated key representatives of selected regional variations of muay to oversee its development. It was only in the late 1920s, with the systemization of regional variations of muay into Muay Thai and the institutionalization of rules and regulations, that "to all intents and purposes, Muay Thai had been born" (Junlakan and Payukvong, 2001: 24).

Despite the historical inaccuracy of the origins of Muay Thai often depicted in popular culture, such narratives are still constantly being perpetuated because such myths constitute one of the pillars upon which the Thai nation myth and the uniqueness of Thai culture are founded. As Vail (1998: 88) eloquently concludes, the "historical tradition of Muay Thai is enriched and ultimately conflated with notions of the Thai Warrior Spirit, *cakravartin* kinship, war, and ideas of nations associated with these same elements."

Bibliography

Allan, D. (2002). Two boys enter, two men leave. A night in Bangkok's Kickboxing Thunderdome, *Journal of Asian Martial Arts*, 11(3), 40–49.

Delp, C. (2005). *Muay Thai basics: Introductory Thai boxing techniques*. Berkeley, California: Blue Snake Books.

Junlakan, L., and Prayukvong, K. (2001). *Muay Thai: A living legacy*. Bangkok: Spry Publishing.

Krauss, E., and Cordoza, G., with Yingwitayakhun, T. (2006). *Muay Thai unleashed: Learn technique and strategy from Thailand's warrior elite*. New York: McGraw Hill.

Muay Thai Institute. Background and history of Muay Thai. http://www.muaythai-institute.net/html/history.html (accessed 5 April 2011).

Skaggs, J. (2003). Daily life at a Muay Thai boxing camp, *Journal of Asian Martial Arts*, 12(4), 49–64.

Thongchai, W. (1994). *Siam mapped: A history of the geo-body of a nation*. Honolulu: The University Press of Hawaii.

Vail, P. (1998). Modern Muay Thai mythology. *Crossroads: An interdisciplinary Journal of Southeast Asia Studies*, 12(2), 75–95.

Wit, T. (2001). *Se-Ed's modern Thai-English dictionary*. Bangkok: Se-Ed Education Public Company.

chapter 6

An Exploration of the Bando System and Other Ancient Burmese Fighting Traditions: History and Current Practices

by Duvon G. Winborne, Ph.D.

Statue of King Bayint Naungo of Myanmar.
©123RF Stock Photo. *Photo by Narongsak Nagadhana.*

Introduction

What is the nature of *bando* (pronounced bawn'doh)? Bando is an ancient Pali word that meant self-discipline, self-development, and self-improvement during the third to ninth centuries CE. The meaning of bando evolved since those earlier centuries to denote self-protection, self-guard, or self-defense against various forms of threat. As a practical matter, the term bando was chosen as a substitute for the Burmese term *thaing*, because bando was easier to pronounce in English and had greater semantic adherence to martial arts systems beyond the Burmese region (e.g., aikido, judo, kendo). The two terms, bando and thaing, should be thought of as synonymous relative to reflecting the comprehensive system of Burmese combative arts (Draeger and Smith, 1989; Gyi, 1989). The modern version of bando is organized into three subsystems—*dha* (edged-weapon techniques), *dhot* (staff-weapon techniques), and *dhoe* (empty-hand techniques).

The recent history of bando owes much to the insights of the late U Ba Than Gyi and his colleagues, who formed the Military Athletics Club in the central region of the country currently known as the Republic of the Union of Myanmar. Saya Gyi, whose military name was Bawanje Rai, served in the early 1900s as a military officer of the 10th Burma Gurkha Rifles (*saya* means teacher or master).

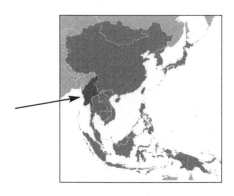

Location of Burma, today known as Myanmar.

He was successful in efforts to restore and modernize the ancient fighting systems that were endemic of the Burmese region. Although many of Saya Gyi's initiatives were driven by a strong cultural imperative, the spread of global conflict during the 1930s and 1940s significantly led to the development of Hanthawaddy bando.

Certain basic techniques of the bando system were used to prepare young Burmese men for combat during World War II. U Ba Than Gyi eventually became one of the founders of the National Bando Association and passed his profound martial arts legacy to his son, Dr. Maung Gyi.

In the late 1950s, Maung Gyi introduced a traditional Burmese fighting system to the United States martial arts community. The American martial arts scene at that time was dominated by grappling systems from Japan, and the increasingly popular striking systems from Okinawa and Korea. There was even some familiarity with the flowing and circular movements of Chinese martial arts, largely due to the influx of Chinese migrants to communities along the Eastern Seaboard and West Coast. Few practitioners were aware of the unique system of bando, which is closely associated with the Gurkhas of India, Nepal, and, of course, Myanmar. Dr. Gyi was one of the early proponents of Southeast Asian martial systems, teaching bando in the United States a decade or more before some other systems from the Philippines, Thailand, Indonesia, and Malaysia (Winborne, 1995).

On 15 June 1967, Maung Gyi formed the American Bando Association (ABA) at Ohio University, where he held a faculty position in psycholinguistics. The ABA was formed primarily to preserve the ancient Burmese fighting traditions and to esteem other martial arts systems emanating from the Southeast Asian region. In accordance with its mission, the ABA is a nonprofit organization that actively honors armed services veterans and provides volunteer support to veterans-related institutions. Special emphasis is placed on recognizing contributions of the 10th Burma Gurkha Rifles (1766–1966) and acknowledging those individuals who fought in the China-Burma-India Theater of World War II. The ABA is one of the longest-existing martial arts organizations in the country.

Similar to other comprehensive martial arts systems, the range of techniques, methods, and approaches in the bando system is expansive. Practitioners develop skills with various types of ancient weapons that were used in historic battles of Burma. The short sword known as the *khukuri* is the seminal edged weapon of bando, yet many practitioners are skillful with long swords (*dhas*), spears, daggers, and other traditional implements. Staff methods in bando focus on the battlefield-tested long staff, which ranges in length from nine to twelve feet, and other staffs, including the military-style baton, the monk staff, and combat sticks of short lengths. Empty-hand methods of bando are most often derived from the nine animal fighting systems that feature both striking grappling and striking combat tactics. The combat sports of letway and naban are two additional ancient Burmese traditions. There is even the high style of bando, defined as the monk system, which focuses on nonviolent self-defense and healing methods. Each of these aspects of bando will be discussed in this chapter.

Roots of Bando

Unlike other systems popularized during the past half century or more, Burmese bando continues to maintain a shroud of mystique in America and Europe. Bando is, however, a well-tested system of combat techniques and fitness training rooted in the ancient tribal cultures of Myanmar, India, and Nepal—particularly reflected in the exploits of Gurkhas soldiers. Gurkhas established their combat renown in the sixteenth century through fierce battles against the British military (Cross and Gurung, 2002). Known for their endurance and blade skills, the Gurkhas have distinguished themselves in battles ranging from the Pindaree War of 1817 to the Falkland War of 1982, to even the more recent conflicts within Afghanistan and Kosova. Gurkha regiments continue to serve as adjunct support for the British military, based on a peace accord signed at Sugauli in 1816.

Bando has as much depth as other fighting arts originating in China or Japan, but the isolationist policies of the Burmese government have severely hampered cultural exchanges with Western countries. Notwithstanding politics, the philosophy and practices of the Burmese fighting arts found their way to Western nations, including France, Canada, Great Britain, and the United States, primarily through the efforts of Dr. Maung Gyi. To grasp more fully the development of bando in the US, it seems prudent to explore the pioneering efforts of Maung Gyi and the martial arts vision imparted to him by his father, U Ba Than Gyi.

Bah Than Gyi sits in meditation.
He is Dr. Maung Gyi's father and prime influence.

The elder Gyi served as an officer of the 10th Burma Gurkha Rifles, and was formally educated in linguistics and physiology. Ba Than Gyi formed the Military Athletics Club in Maymaya, Burma, during the mid-1900s, with the support of colleagues from the Burmese military (Winborne, 1995). He was successful in efforts to restore and modernize the ancient fighting systems endemic to the region, including systems from Tibet and China.

While the elder Gyi's initiatives were driven by a strong cultural imperative, the spread of global conflict during the late 1930s and early 1940s significantly influenced bando's development. The real threat of a Japanese incursion during World War II forced Burmese officials to seek an efficient combat system that would work on the battlefield. Ba Than Gyi helped to streamline the ancient bando system and incorporated its methods into an effective military training regimen. Certain basic techniques of bando were taught to young Burmese military recruits, who were preparing for combat during that period. Fighting methods deemed esoteric or impractical were modified to improve functionality, giving way to a modernized version of bando.

Ba Than Gyi believed in seeking techniques that worked and discarded any martial elements that were not practical. The elder Gyi likened the modernized version of Hanthawaddy bando to a dump truck. This description was offered as a contrast to many other martial arts styles with highly complex and sophisticated movements. These other styles were viewed by Ba Than Gyi as analogous to a fine sports car, such as a Maserati or Lamborghini. In contrast, he explained bando as a utility-oriented vehicle that would be "durable under stress like a dump truck" (Gyi, 1989, p. 84). By the start of World War II, the bando system had been structured into a set of functional methods, which were adopted and codified from many sources throughout Southeast Asia.

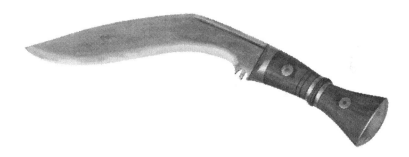

A khukuri — the seminal
edged weapon of bando.

The elder Gyi, Ba Than, invited martial arts masters from China, India, and Tibet to share their fighting techniques and strategies with the Burmese. Maung Gyi and two other young scholars were given responsibility for studying and documenting the various styles displayed by the invited masters. Approaches for edged weapons and staffs were presented by Chinese practitioners, and Indian masters shared highly effective grappling methods. The techniques of animal systems fighting from Tibet and southern China were also prominently explored during these postwar years (Gyi, 2000b). Ba Than Gyi carefully guided the development process, ensuring that only functional elements from these diverse approaches would be incorporated into a modernized bando system. His military background and recent war experiences ensured that bando would remain a practical system. Nevertheless, the elder Gyi held firm to a philosophy that "just as no one Nation has a monopoly on sunlight, no one system has a monopoly on truth . . ." (p. 160). This axiom continues to influence bando's evolution, even in the twenty-first century.

Journeyman Maung Gyi

Many superlatives are appropriate when qualifying the lifelong accomplishments of Dr. Maung Gyi, whose innovations, intellect, and influences make him the exception that defines the rule of martial arts pioneer. Consider for a moment the fact that Maung Gyi changed the martial arts landscape of America when he introduced his unique Burmese combat system, known as bando, to the US over fifty years ago. It is useful to understand the enlightened journey that brought Gyi and bando to the States.

Dr. Maung Gyi stands with champion students John Taylor,
Laszlo Balogh, Bob Hill, and Bob Maxwell at the USKA
National Tournament in Chicago, Illinois, 1965.

In the early 1940s, young Maung Gyi faced extreme disappointment as his dreams of becoming a physician faded. Political conflicts between his native Burma and the imperialistic Japanese leadership led to a war between the two nations. All adult males in the Gyi family joined the Burmese military during World War II, and there were casualties among them. Uncles, cousins, and even Maung Gyi's brother were killed in battle (Rai and Kufus, 1992). Recruited to serve in a Gurkha regiment, the youthful Gyi spent some of his military service as a medic, which continued to fuel his ambitions for a medical career. His fate, however, shifted dramatically when Maung Gyi was forced to defend himself against Japanese soldiers while attempting to aid fallen comrades on the battlefield. During this phase of life Maung Gyi benefitted directly from his father's insights regarding the applicability of bando techniques. With khukuri in hand, he fought in dark trenches, jungle thickets, and hilly terrains against armed opponents. The rule was "kill as many of them as possible before they kill us," and Gyi chose survival (Rai and Kufus, 1992, p. 58).

The Japanese were armed with katanas and bayonets, while the Burmese soldiers used their short curved swords (*khukuris*) to fend off the foreign invaders. The young Maung Gyi had received instruction on combat uses of the khukuri during military basic training. He honed his sword skills on the battlefield and developed a keen sensibility for pragmatics in the martial arts. Daggers, swords, long staffs, and other handheld weapons were used in battle by Gyi during the Japanese incursion (Rai and Kufus, 1994). The need to survive forced him to learn combat techniques quickly and efficiently. British military historians and archivists have, in fact, credited Maung Gyi with several battlefield kills during World War II.

The martial arts training not only continued but intensified for Maung Gyi in the years immediately following World War II. Still in his early twenties, Maung Gyi worked closely with his father and other combat veterans to document various elements of bando. Particular attention was paid to integrating higher-order skills into a comprehensive fighting system that would reflect both the vision of Ba Than Gyi and the diverse martial techniques of the Burmese region—particularly the animal fighting styles (Winborne and Gyi, 1995). Principles and practices learned from martial arts masters were carefully recorded and organized into an evolved bando system.

While Maung Gyi was influenced by many fighting approaches to which he was exposed, there grew within him a profound interest in the cobra system. He spent an extended period living with an actual cobra system master who raised the poisonous snakes for their venom. Maung Gyi would subsequently become a cobra system master himself and teach the system to others. Unable to ignore the warrior spirit within, he also delved deeply into techniques of the bull and boar systems, effectively integrating certain approaches into the sport of letway (more about this sport will be presented later). The youthful Gyi competed in dozens of matches against fighters throughout Southeast Asia, including Thailand, Laos, and Malaysia. Eventually, he became a champion fighter and gained international recognition for his skill.

Maung Gyi moved to the United States in the late 1950s. His primary purposes for relocating were to pursue higher education and to support the humanitarian efforts of his uncle, the late U Thant, who served as Secretary-General of the United Nations from 1962 to 1971. Although employment and educational opportunities attracted Maung Gyi to the States, advancement of the bando system may well have been the compelling force that kept him in America. Shifting his energy away from survival and competition, he enrolled in several prestigious institutions—including Johns Hopkins and Harvard Universities—subsequently attaining both law and doctoral degrees. While working as a linguist in Washington, DC, Maung Gyi introduced a modified version of the bando system to a few select students in 1960. He also trained Secret Service personnel, FBI staff, and security officials during this phase.

A few years later, he organized the first bando club in the States at the American University in DC. Many students were attracted to bando because of the uniqueness of this Gurkha-based fighting style, which preceded some of the other Southeast Asian arts in the US by decades (Winborne, 1995). Methods of the bando system contrasted sharply with those of the popular Japanese and Korean styles, which dominated the martial arts scene, and practitioners were impressed with the speed and efficiency of Gyi's techniques. Throughout the Eastern Seaboard, Gyi entered his students into karate tournaments and forms competitions. These early students, clad in nontra-ditional black uniforms, often dominated their matches and captured many titles. Shinbone kicks, leaping punches, and knee blocks were nearly unknown outside of bando, and Maung Gyi's early students applied these techniques effectively against other stylists.

Dr. Gyi demonstrates his powerful and accurate side kick technique during a tournament in Cleveland, Ohio, 1969.

However, the tournament exploits of Maung Gyi himself were nothing short of mystical. He was known to "move like a cat," according to author and tai chi master Robert Smith. When performing, Gyi's sidekicks were executed with such grace and precision that audiences frequently cheered and applauded. His long-staff techniques flowed with a speed that made the staff nearly imperceptible.

That is, the staff seemed to disappear from Dr. Gyi's hands, only to reappear with devastating accuracy and power. While expressing the need for a good quality fighting staff, Gyi decried the strength of many commercial products and systematically demonstrated his point. One by one, he shattered a pile of commercially produced fighting staffs by striking them against a tree, using the same technique.

His movements seemed effortless, yet the staffs splintered upon impact. Several bando practitioners who witnessed the event described the performance as magical and proclaimed Gyi's uncanny martial arts abilities (Draeger and Smith, 1989; Winborne, 1995). Having mastered the cobra system, Maung Gyi was periodically invited to offer public demonstrations of the rarely seen animal system. A primary offensive technique of this animal style is the cobra strike, which simulates a cobra's venomous bite against its prey. To illustrate the effectiveness of this type of strike, Gyi had an assistant toss several inflated balloons into the air. In rapid succession, Gyi struck the free-falling balloons with a single cobra strike, causing them to burst.

Everett Givens practices evasion techniques and footwork drills during a bama letway training session in Athens, Ohio, September 1995.

His hands moved with such speed that the actual strikes could not be seen. It gave the illusion that the balloons were bursting on their own. Observers of the demonstration were mesmerized, almost incapable of processing what they were witnessing. Such demonstrations fostered the mystique of Maung Gyi and his art of bando—a mystique that continues to this day. Garnering the attention and acknowledgment of other pioneers in the US, Dr. Gyi had become a leader and innovator in various areas of the martial arts. He was well respected by all the prominent masters who helped to shape martial arts practices in America, including Ed Parker (kenpo), Mas Oyama (Kyokushinkai), Harold Long (Isshinryu), Robert Trias (Shuri-ryu), Mas Oshima (Shotokan), and Jhoon Rhee (taekwondo). These early accomplishments of Dr. Maung Gyi were a testament to his skill and intellect. He served as chief referee for most major karate tournaments throughout the country, and chaired the Tournament Rules Committee for *Black Belt* magazine, which established a point system for karate matches.

Many of the early karate matches refereed by Gyi involved noted champions, including Mike Stone, Chuck Norris, Bill Wallace, Joe Lewis, and Tom LaPuppet (Winborne, 1995; Winborne and Gyi, 1995).

Bama Letway & Bando Boxing

For centuries an unarmed combat sport has been practiced in Burma among the various tribes and ethnic groups. This ancient sport was known in the Burmese language as bama letway (Burmese boxing). Two fighters would enter a large dirt circle for issuing challenges to one another, through a rhythmic dance defined as the *letway yei*. Matches between fighters were not timed, and there were no weight classes. These early contests allowed for the use of nearly all empty-hand fighting techniques, including kicks, punches, throws, traps, and even head butts.

Men versed in the sport of bama letway competed without head protection, and the hands and feet were usually bare. A folded triangular garment was wrapped around each fighter's waist, decorated in the color and patterns of his village or tribe, and the combatants adorned their arms with sacred amulets. Protective equipment was limited to coconut shells for groin guards, and strips of leather were placed in the mouth to shield the teeth. Musicians played up-tempo melodies for these outdoor matches to stimulate fighters toward frenzied combat (Gyi, 2000b).

Each contestant was represented by two referees who were responsible for upholding the bama letway rules. These four referees were expected to separate the fighters after a clinch, throw, or trapping technique. Also, there was a chief referee assigned to intervene if any problems arose during the matches. Victory was determined when one of the contestants (1) bled profusely from a facial or body cut; (2) yielded because of a broken limb or joint dislocation; or (3) was rendered unconscious from a strike, throw, or other technique.

From the reign of King Anawratha in 1044 to the nineteenth-century transition period, Burmese men and boys trained diligently on the skills of bama letway to reap financial rewards and regional fame. However, the practice of this ancient combat sport was not limited to the boarders of Burma, but rather spread to neighboring territories, regional conflicts, and invasions. The kingdoms of Siam (Thailand), Laos, Mon, Shan, Kayin, and Assam were all subjugated by the Burmese King Bayainnaung as he created an expansive empire in 1551. The reign of this king during the sixteenth century represented the historic height of Burma's influence over Southeast Asia and beyond. During this era, King Bayainnaung promoted numerous bama letway matches throughout his empire and established standard rules for the popular combat sport (Gyi, 2000b; Winborne, 2011).

A notable event of this sixteenth-century period was the nurturing of the Siamese prince Naresuan, who was taken to Burma as a young boy. Under the watchful eyes of his adoptive father, King Bayainnaung, the prince was trained in bama letway, weapons, and horsemanship. The Siamese prince displayed uncanny fighting abilities and developed into a fierce warrior. Years later, the adult Prince Naresuan would return to his homeland and successfully lead an army against Burma to reestablish the independence of Siam (Rashidi and Van Sertima, 1985; Black, 2005). Known historically as the "Black Prince," Naresuan introduced bama letway as part of military training in Siam, and he is credited as a major influence on the development of Muay Thai as a combat sport in modern-day Thailand (Winborne, 2011, p. 11).

Left: Dillon Hayman executes a leaping
knee attack against Anthony Vionet in
a bando boxing demonstration match.
Right: Richard Gray serves as referee
at the Smithsonian Institute Folklife
Festival in Washington, DC, July 4, 2010.

During the British rule of Burma, the infrastructure of bama letway was decimated. Various criminal codes imposed by the British government prohibited the practice of bama letway and other martial arts systems in Burma. In fact, bando practitioners were classified as habitual criminals and vagrants in the early decades of the 1900s. Thai boxing, by contrast, grew in popularity as a national sport during this same period, supported by the king of Thailand, the Ministry of Sports and Athletics, and large businesses. The traditional art of bama letway made its successful transition to modernity through the successful adaption of Western Queensbury boxing rules.

Noting Thailand's success, Ba Than Gyi believed the traditional Burmese combat sport could be restored by adopting Western boxing rules and by enhancing safety practices for fighters. He implemented modifications to bama letway that proved effective in reducing serious injuries to competitors. The newly configured sport was defined as bando boxing in 1950. Saya Gyi held the post of director of physical education, sports, and athletics, and promoted bando boxing to a new generation of students enrolled in schools and colleges nationwide. Keenly aware of potential health benefits, Ba Than Gyi promoted high-level athletic competitions at the amateur and professional ranks, understanding that training requirements for such events would improve overall fitness levels of male youths in Burma (Gyi, 1989). Similar results had been observed in neighboring Thailand, where ancient bama letway was successfully transformed into the modern sport of Muay Thai.

What were some of these Western modifications of bama letway that led to the current sport of bando boxing? Safety equipment and weight classes were incorporated into the modern version of the sport. Amateur competitors were required to wear head protection, rubber mouth guards, boxing gloves, and other protective gear. Depending on age and experience, boxers were able to compete within the novice class, senior class, or open class. Weight divisions were created for competitors in ten-pound groups, starting at 90–99 lbs. for lightweight fighters and progressing to the super heavyweight division of 240 lbs. or greater. The age groupings for fighters began at the level of 11–12 years old and increased to the terminal level of 46–50 years old.

In bando boxing there were three rounds for each match, with a round lasting two minutes. Contests took place in a Western-style boxing ring with a canvas floor. There was a referee within the ring to manage the contest, intervening when boxers clashed, clinched, or attempted illegal techniques. Five side judges evaluated each round in accordance with the ten-point must system of scoring. In this system, the winner of a round received ten points, and the loser received eight or nine points. The ultimate winner of a match was determined by (1) the boxer with the highest number of points, (2) an actual knockout or technical knockout, (3) the voluntary retirement or withdrawal of a boxer, or (4) a judgment of match disqualification by the referee for illegal technique(s).

Having gained increased popularity among young men in Burma, the long tradition of combat sport was revitalized through insightful developments of U Ba Than Gyi. Moreover, the centuries-old Burmese tradition was amply represented in the pioneering efforts of his son in America. Maung Gyi was well versed in both sports of bando boxing and Western boxing (Winborne, 2011). As a former Olympic boxer, the younger Gyi competed successfully in professional boxing matches in New York and New Jersey, periodically knocking out heavyweight opponents. What is most impressive about these matches is the weight differential. He weighed between 140 and 145 pounds at the time and only fought against light heavyweight and heavyweight opponents.

With over ninety bama letway and Muay Thai matches to his credit from the formative years in Burma, Maung Gyi introduced the sport of kickboxing to the US. He organized the first full-contact bando boxing contest in Washington, DC, during 1960. Maung Gyi was well aware of how Western boxing techniques could radically augment and improve bando and other Asian fighting systems (Winborne, 1995).

Dr. Gyi poses with a large contingent of bando students from
West Virginia, Ohio, Maryland, Pennsylvania, and Washington, DC,
following a rigorous weekend in kickboxing training camp
at Buffalo Gap Campgrounds, West Virginia, summer 1971.

Full-Contact Sparring in America

When Maung Gyi began teaching bando in the late 1950s, he remained pure to the early traditions of animal systems, bama letway, naban, and other components of the system. His approach was raw, uncut, and novel. Over time, he began teaching bando at the American University in Washington, DC, where restrictions were placed on his martial arts instruction. University officials disallowed training sessions with staff weapons and edged weapons. Moreover, Maung Gyi was not permitted to teach the modified combat sport of bando boxing or even to train students in Western boxing. Modifications were made in the bando curriculum to comply with university guidelines (Winborne, 2011). Sparring methods were adjusted for light-contact and noncontact tournament competition. Despite these restrictions, many training sessions remained true to the rugged fighting traditions of Burma. Bare-knuckle competitions were held behind closed doors among willing practitioners. Frequently, these raw matches resulted in bleeding, bruises, and broken bones for the fighters. Some students from these early days of bando training at the American University would eventually become successful kickboxing and tournament fighters, as well as great martial arts teachers. In the late 1960s, Maung Gyi moved to Athens, Ohio, for academic and career pursuits. He obtained a position at Ohio University as professor of psycholinguistics and communications. Bando students from Washington, DC, and Maryland continued training with Gyi in Athens. Yet there was an influx of new students who hailed from Ohio, West Virginia, and Pennsylvania. The environment of Ohio University was highly conducive to developing the refined art of bando boxing. Maung Gyi purchased a farm in rural southeast Ohio, where his students could experience many of the rigorous training methods used in Burma.

There were no institutional restrictions on the Gyi farm—just raw bando training (Gyi, 2000b). Various fitness and body-hardening drills were taught and practitioners were able to experience full-contact sparring. The techniques of blocking, stepping, slipping, and angling were practiced routinely for good defensive fighting. Further, heavy bags, speed bags, and pads were used to develop powerful offensive techniques.

Practitioners were increasing their skills, yet there were few opportunities for bando practitioners to compete in full-contact matches. Some bando students opted for joining the Ohio University boxing club, where Dr. Gyi had assumed the role of head coach. However, the ultimate solution was the establishment of an Annual National Bando Amateur Kickboxing Tournament in 1971. This was the beginning of full-contact tournament competition for martial arts in America. Based on Western Queensbury boxing rules adopted years before by his father in Burma, Maung Gyi sponsored the first kickboxing tournament in southeast Ohio with bando practitioners and martial artists from other systems.

Left: Anthony Vionet executes a classic shin kick to the midsection of Dillon Hayman during a demonstration kickboxing match. Right: Dillon Hayman and Anthony Vionet clash during the same match. Match referee was Richard Gray for this contest held at the Smithsonian Institute Folklife Festival in Washington, DC, July 4, 2010.

Over the years, the bando kickboxing tournament has grown in size and prominence, attracting martial artists nationwide and from several foreign countries. The year 2011 marked the fortieth anniversary of the tournament, which remains the longest-running full-contact martial arts tournament in America (Gyi, 2000b; Winborne, 2011). During the past four decades the event has been held each Veterans Day weekend in varied locations, including Athens, Ohio; Wheeling, West Virginia; and Columbus, Ohio. Open to other systems, participants in this annual event have represented Japanese karate, Chinese gongfu, Thai boxing, Korean taekwondo, Indonesian silat, Okinawan karate, Filipino kali, and, of course, bando boxing. In recent years a growing number of mixed martial arts practitioners have entered the bando kickboxing tournament.

Free Fighting & Forms
Focusing back on the early days, the martial arts scene in America was dominated by Japanese, Chinese, Korean, and Okinawan systems. Burmese bando was the only system from Southeast Asia at that time. Instructors and practitioners from Thailand, Malaysia, Indonesia, and other countries of the region would reach the States years later. Bando fighters entered open karate tournaments throughout the Eastern Seaboard and Midwest region of the US

in order to gain mainstream acceptance. However, many practitioners of bando experienced difficulty with adjusting to the predominant point system of judging used in most tournaments. Participation in karate matches often resulted in disqualifications and tournament ejections (Gyi, 2000b).

Dr. Maung Gyi stands with students (standing) Bob Vanne, Andy Hessman, Gen Lai Chen, Hugh McHugh, (kneeling) Little Andy, Masahito Nashida, Yuteka Nashida, Paul Kwan, and unknowns who won sparring and forms competitions in an open tournament (circa 1964).

Bando tournaments feature round-robin competition and continuous fighting. Al Graves and Mark Simmonson spar for a gold medal, May 1998, in Alexandria, Virginia.

The Burmese approach to sparring focused on continuous fighting between two opponents for a period of two or three minutes without interruption. Sparring techniques were often derived from bando's animal systems, including the use of elbows, knees, forearms, and shin bones. Traditional approaches also focused on nerve strikes, throwing methods, trapping strategies, and leaping skills derived from animal systems. Drastic adjustments were necessary for bando fighters to conform to rules established by tournament organizers (Gyi, 2000b). Some fighters made successful adjustment in their techniques to curry favor with karate-oriented judges, but a large number of bando practitioners were unable to modify their skills for point-system sparring (Mitchell, 1988; Miller, 1989).

The need for a venue where bando practitioners could compete with light contact, and continuous sparring, gave birth to the ABA's annual National Free-Fighting Tournament (a.k.a. Middle-Style Tournament). Scheduled on each Memorial Day weekend, the competition has been held annually for more than forty years and maintains the theme of honoring veterans of military service. What are the technical features of free fighting in bando? Fighters are allowed to use an array of kicks, punches, blocks, and other methods associated with the ancient Burmese combat sports and animal systems (Winborne, 1995). This approach enables practitioners to test their fighting skills against opponents in a controlled setting. Appropriate protective equipment must be worn by all competitors, including sparring gloves, mouth guards, head gear, and shin-foot guards.

In contrast to many karate competitions, free-fighting competitors are required to spar against all other competitors within their particular division—a system known as "round robin." Divisions are based on rank, gender, and weight. Contact is permitted, but it must be light and is limited to specific target areas. Each match lasts for two minutes, with the winner determined by a simple majority of ring judges, including the referee's vote. And, competitors with the highest number of wins within each division are awarded first-, second-, and third-place medals.

Competitors who exhibit excessive force are disqualified from the particular match and possibly from the entire competition. Even children are allowed to compete in free fighting, but keen attention is given to sportsmanship and safety for these young bando practitioners. Essentially, the rules of free fighting were established to prevent serious injury while engendering the spirit of ancient Burmese martial sports within bando tournaments throughout the United States.

A second major component of the National Free-Fighting Tournament is the forms competition (i.e., kata), which includes both empty-hand and weapons techniques. All levels of practitioners have an opportunity to display their skills in competitions defined by rank alone.

Black belts in the bando system may compete with forms based on animal systems or advanced combat approaches. The lower-ranking practitioners execute a more fundamental level of fighting techniques, including blocks, strikes, and kicks. Nevertheless, there are certain bando principles that can be seen in all levels of forms, including stepping patterns, body angles, and fighting stances. Such performances are designed to reflect bando principles in a stylistic and exacting fashion.

Edged-weapons techniques are reserved for the more experienced practitioners who have attained the rank of brown belt or black belt. Ever mindful of safety to practitioners and observers, the forms that include the various weapons are taught only to mature, disciplined practitioners. Even staff weapons, including long staffs, batons, and short sticks, are used in such competitions with a high premium placed on safety. Again, only the more experienced bando practitioners are allowed to demonstrate their training and skills with staff weapons. There is also a drill-team competition for edged and staff weapons. Drill teams consist of three or more advanced-ranking practitioners who perform well-coordinated and synchronized routines with weapons or other implements.

Left: Dax Johnson executes a classic bando leap punch against Robin Griffith during a heavyweight free-fighting bout. Right: Gustavo Santos executes a shin kick, as Dax Johnson blocks with a raised knee. Classic bando techniques used during a heavyweight free-fighting bout. Event held in Baltimore, Maryland, May 2013. Kenny Corl is the referee.

Judging of all forms, including drill-team competition, is done by senior ABA members who have a mature understanding of techniques and aesthetics. Forms competitions result in the selection of first-place, second-place, and third-place winners, each receiving a medal or plaque.

Naban: Burmese Wrestling

Naban competitions have gained increasing popularity during the past decade and are often included as a third component of the National Free-Fighting Tournament. Naban is an ancient Burmese grappling sport that has roots in animal systems and the wrestling traditions of the Southeast Asian region. The system can be traced back to the third century CE and it is replete with various grappling methods, including trapping, holding, throwing, locking, tripping, and flipping.

Early developments in naban owed much to the fighting arts of India, Mongolia, China, and Tibet. However, the actual combat sport of naban began to emerge with its own unique identity in Burma after the ninth century CE, following the destruction of the Pagan Empire (Draeger and Smith, 1989; Rashidi, R. and Van Sertima, 1985; Black, 2005).

Later developments in naban are linked with the scholarly efforts of His Holiness Mogok Sayadaw, the venerable Buddhist monk of north-central Burma. Considered the foremost expert of this grappling art in modern history, Mogok Sayadaw discovered ancient manuscripts taken from Burmese temples by foreign traders as he traveled throughout the region. Recovering several manuscripts, the monk was able to codify the philosophy and principles of naban. He taught the fighting system to interested persons at his monastery in Mogok, Burma, during the 1930s. Mogok Sayadaw's students were quite diverse relative to ethnic backgrounds and race, and they were all enrolled in the Teachers Training College of Mandalay. Preservation of the ancient grappling system of naban is almost exclusively credited to this Buddhist monk (Gyi, 2000b).

Rules for a modernized version of naban were based on adaptations of Greco-Roman and Indian wrestling, as Western colonial powers heavily influenced Burmese traditions in the early 1900s. Changes in combat sport rules were implemented to ensure the safety of competitors, as was the case with bama letway. Mogok Sayadaw disclosed documented evidence of several naban competitors having been killed, blinded, and severely maimed during the sixth century CE. Thus, techniques involving biting, eye gouging, hair pulling, clawing, and other animal system strategies were eliminated for the modernized combat sport. Also removed from the ancient version of naban were the techniques of punching, kicking, elbow strikes, and head butting.

Consequently, these rule changes transformed naban from a lethal fighting system to a highly competitive grappling sport.

Few naban experts have survived since the monastic teachings of Mogok Sayadaw over eighty years ago. Despite this obscurity, efforts to preserve these ancient and modernized Burmese traditions have been undertaken by the ABA. Several successful naban competitions have been sponsored by the association during the past decade. Matches are held in gymnasiums and athletic facilities where wrestling mats and padding are available. The matches are timed and competitors are grouped into weight classes. Only adults are permitted to compete in naban tournaments.

Naturally, the customary bando approach of round-robin competitor pairing is used in naban tournaments. As such, martial arts practitioners must prepare for such grappling competitions with rigorous strength and endurance training to ensure success. Points are awarded to competitors for pinning an opponent on his back, side, or stomach for a predetermined amount of time (e.g., 15-30 seconds).

Takedowns, throws, and escapes are also awarded points during the timed matches. A submission hold upon an opponent results in an immediate win, regardless of elapsed time. As with other bando competitions, first-place, second-place, and third-place medals are given to the top three practitioners in each weight class.

Left: John Paul Shelhammer performs a takedown
against Matthew Israel. Right: Israel executes
a full-body throw against Shelhammer.
Richard Gray serves as referee during these
naban system demonstration matches at
an event held at the Smithsonian Institute
Folklife Festival in Washington, DC, July 4, 2010.

Left: Fredi Prevost executes double cobra strikes against Sidney Grandison in Catonsville, Maryland, July 1999. Right: Python system master Rick Rossiter demonstrates ground kicks and traps at a training camp in Athens, Ohio, August 2004. 27

Animal Fighting Systems

Burmese bando was, and remains, as much a tribute to nature as it is an amalgam of ancient and modernized fighting traditions. Early inhabitants of the Southeast Asian region studied survival strategies of the indigenous wild animals to enhance their own prospects for survival in challenging environments. According to Venerable Mogok Sayadaw, various tribes and clans migrated into Burma from the Himalayan regions around 1000 BCE. These early inhabitants worshiped nature, practiced Shamanism, and carefully observed wild animals to learn important lessons about survival. From these observations, combat systems were developed that emulated the hunting and defensive tactics of animals in the wild (Gyi, 2000a).

Over the centuries as many as thirty animal fighting systems evolved and were practiced throughout Burma. Formal documentation was limited and many of these systems disappeared during British colonial rule, particularly the period following WWII. Nevertheless, Ba Than Gyi preserved and systematized and passed the knowledge to his son Maung Gyi. There were twelve such fighting systems based on indigenous wild animals that were practiced by martial arts students under the tutelage of Ba Than Gyi, three of which were excluded from the evolved bando system fostered in the US (Winborne, 1995). Specifically, the boar, bull, cobra, eagle, python, panther, tiger, viper, and scorpion animal fighting systems have been preserved by the ABA (the deer, monkey, and paddy bird were excluded). Maung Gyi carefully selected nine bando students to learn the philosophy, principles, and practices of each bando animal fighting system. Having studied intensely for twenty or more years, the selected students became highly proficient in the fighting methods of their respective disciplines, resulting in the designation of animal system masters by Maung Gyi in 2003.

What are some unique techniques of each bando animal fighting system? The cobra and viper systems feature striking techniques that simulate disabling venom. Viper system techniques involve powerful strikes that are generated from compression of the practitioner's body. Movements are like coiled springs, striking with hardened fingers, knuckles, and half fists at target areas. Such blows may readily break bones. In contrast, cobra system techniques involve straightening, raising, and twisting the body to deliver strikes. Practitioners use circular motions to locate targets and to deliver blows with hardened fingers, knuckles, and half fists. Aimed at nerve centers, cobra system blows often slash, cut, and penetrate skin (Winborne and Anderson, 2000).

The tiger and panther systems both reflect strategies of large predatory felines. Combat approaches of both systems are similar, with the panther considered a smaller version of the tiger. Movements involve jumping, spinning, rolling, and flurries of strikes. Practitioners of the tiger and panther systems must be strong, flexible, and agile to execute sweeps to fell opponents during combat. Strikes of these feline systems are delivered with the hands and feet (Winborne and Gyi, 1998).

Bull and boar systems are considered to be hard approaches to combat, requiring greater strength and size than other animal fighting systems of bando. Boars are smaller versions of bulls, yet both animals have the general physical structure of strong necks, broad shoulders, large arms and legs, and wide girth. Practitioners of both the bull and boar systems use rushing charges to deliver strikes with elbows, knees, fists, and head butts. Close-range combat is required in both systems. Interestingly, many elements from these two fighting systems were adapted for use in bando boxing and free fighting (Scherban and Nightingale, 1986; Kufus, 1993).

Movements of the eagle system involve circular and straight patterns to emulate the wings of raptors. Eagle system practitioners use both hands simultaneously or alternately when blocking or striking. In fact, more than 90 percent of the movements in this fighting system are made with two hands. The beak, wings, and talons are emulated by the hands of eagle system practitioners for striking opponents. Such strikes stun, hold, tear, and break various targets in combat (Hyder and Menard, 1996).

Bando's python system employs throws, hold, and strikes during combat. Grappling methods of the python system are similar to those found in Japanese styles (e.g., judo, jujitsu), except grabs are done on the opponent's hair, face, skin, ears, and fingers. Python system practitioners often slam or drop opponents, followed with combat locks to the face, neck, arms, legs, or spine (Gyi, 2000b).

The scorpion is considered a living fossil, as the species has survived for millions of years. This particular animal fighting system of bando is enshrouded in mystique, based on traditional cultural aversions and superstitions. Nevertheless, the scorpion system is an effective fighting approach that incorporates evasive footwork, seizing techniques, and ground combat to attack nerve centers of opponents. The major approaches of this unique fighting system are trapping, pinching, and stinging. Once an opponent is trapped, the scorpion system practitioner will pluck, pierce, or puncture nerve centers to cause pain and convulsions (Winborne, 1994).

These nine animal fighting systems of bando have various levels of applications and practice, including attendant weapons strategies, rituals, forms, and even healing methods. In addition to the designated animal system masters, there are many practitioners in bando who have studied the systems and who have attained high skill levels, thereby preserving the ancient Burmese traditions.

Unique Bando Weapons

Most martial systems throughout the world are comprehensive in structure, featuring a myriad of strategies for staff and edged weapons. Bando is no exception to this rule. Early inhabitants of ancient Burma used ropes, heavy stones, spears, long staffs, and other implements for hunting, farming, and various other domestic tasks. Inevitably, these domestic uses were converted into combat applications when regional conflicts arose. Ba Than Gyi was adamant about preserving the ancient fighting traditions of Burma, and he systematically documented staff and edged-weapons approaches. As discussed earlier, he and his colleagues incorporated several weapons into the Hanthawaddy bando system following World War II (Winborne, 1995). Practitioners in the US have preserved many weapons traditions of the Myanmar region with the guidance of Maung Gyi. Some of the weapons approaches are similar to those used in other martial arts systems from China, Japan, Korea, and other countries. There are, however, three salient weapons that uniquely characterize the bando system and are worthy of discussion herein: the long staff, the khukuri, and the Burmese dha.

Long staff weapons in bando have a proud history that results from combat success during ancient wars. Historians have determined that Kublai Khan (1216-1294) withdrew from Southeast Asia after only a brief occupation.

Battle strategies and long-staff techniques used by ancient Burmese warriors may have contributed significantly to the early withdrawal. Khan led an army of 150,000 mounted soldiers on a campaign designed to conquer the lands that now comprise Burma, Thailand, and other Southeast Asian countries (Nicolle, 1990; Marshall, 1993). Rugged tribesmen of northern Burma developed a highly efficient combat strategy to defeat Khan's horsemen. Using sturdy long staffs of nine feet or more, the Burmese fighters performed strategic strikes to the legs of oncoming warhorses that immediately felled both animal and rider. The powerful type of hardwood staff used during these battles is known in bando as a bull staff. Once grounded, the Mongols lost their combat advantage and were forced to engage in man-to-man combat with the skillful Burmese warriors (Winborne and Gyi, 1997).

Left: Sidney Grandison and Fredi Prevost perform a dha form.
Right: Slashing and shielding techniques are combined with evasive footwork and body angles to create a comprehensive sword-fighting system. Event held at the Smithsonian Institute Folklife Festival in Washington, DC, July 4, 2010.

Combat techniques used during the thirteenth century CE have been incorporated in the ABA's curriculum. Long-staff fighting begins with the fundamental elements of stance, grip, and hold. Bando practitioners are taught to strike and block with the staff, using a process of muscle contraction and controlled breathing referred to as body locking. Training sessions with the long staff focus on coordinated stepping patterns and robust stances that support striking and blocking motions.

Hard targets are often struck to condition the hands, arms, and legs for combat. Also, there are several long-staff forms practiced by ABA members that simulate battlefield combat. These aesthetic forms pay homage to the ancient Burmese warriors of antiquity and preserve the combat legacy. Yet there are other martial benefits to long-staff training. Bando practitioners are keenly aware of empty-hand fighting methods that can be gleaned from long-staff techniques. Trapping, striking, grappling, shielding, and other empty-hand techniques are readily learned from the long staff (Winborne, 1995; Winborne and Gyi, 1997). There are also the added physical fitness benefits of improved strength and stamina derived from repetitive swinging motions with the heavy long staffs of bando.

Left: Duvon Winborne uses double khukuri techniques to counter a long-staff attack by Everett Givens during a training session in Lexington, Kentucky, in 1995. One khukuri is used for shielding while the second blade slashes, cuts, chops, or thrusts the opponent. Right: Rick Rossiter, Al Cook, and Terrell LaTour practice blocking drills during a training seminar with the short staff. Such techniques are useful for military personnel, security specialists, and law enforcement officers, Athens, Ohio, September 1997.

Left: Ancient Burmese warriors used sturdy bull staffs to repel invading Mongol horsemen. Tom Hogan, William Cain, Mark Simmonson, Al Cook, Rick Rossiter, and Jerry George practice thrusting techniques, Athens, Ohio, June 1998.

The khukuri is one of the most celebrated edged weapons in military history. Considered a short sword, the khukuri serves as the iconic symbol for the ABA and is carried during all formal ceremonies. An often misunderstood weapon, the khukuri was used effectively in some of the fiercest battling among ground troops in modern warfare. Ba Than Gyi and his son Maung Gyi were both members of the revered Burma Gurkha Regiment during World War II, and both men used the khukuri in actual battles. Thus, there is a strong legacy for the sword in bando based on cultural and combat relevance (Gyi, 2000b).

It is helpful to consider the khukuri's history. During the mid-eighteenth century CE, Prithi Narayan Sah, the King of Gookha, and his successors conquered an area that is present-day Nepal. Sah led a series of bloody campaigns against the British East India Company, which ultimately led to the signing of a peace treaty with Great Britain in 1816. Since that period, the British have recruited Gurkha soldiers from various Mongoloid Tibetu-Burman-speaking groups, and non-Mongolian clans (Winborne, 1996; Cross and Gurung, 2002; Caplan, 2009). Some military historians suggest that Gurkhas had no special training with the khukuri, but rather adapted their combat skills from various survival tasks, including chopping firewood, butchering meat, hammering nails, and clearing foliage. Although such survival tasks fostered skills, the claims ignore the reality that no military weapon has ever been applied successfully without organized training to support its use (Rai and Kufus, 1992; Rai and Kufus, 1994).

Maung Gyi was the enlightened beneficiary of khukuri training from many highly skilled swordsmen of the World War II period, including his father Ba Than Gyi. These khukuri experts demonstrated effective applications for night combat, close-quarter fighting, and jungle warfare. Senior bando practitioners in the US are commonly versed in safety principles and fighting methods for the khukuri.

Defensive techniques cover a range of blocks, parries, and traps. Parrying and blocking may be accomplished with the blade's sides and back, with trapping techniques involving the sides and front of the khukuri. Offensive strategies for the short sword focus on chopping, slashing, thrusting, butting, cutting, and slapping. Footwork and body angling are also incorporated into the overall skills repertoire for khukuri fighting. Moreover, Maung Gyi has taught a series of aesthetic forms and combat drills that have often been showcased at ABA events, martial arts tournaments, and weapons seminars (Winborne, 1996).

The Burmese dha is a third weapon that is uniquely associated with the bando system. Broad use of long bladed weapons may be noted in various

Southeast Asian cultures. In fact, the term "dha" is generally used to denote an array of knives and swords throughout Indochina. Diversity notwithstanding, the bando system has incorporated the Burmese version of a moderately curved long sword into its curriculum. In structure, the Burmese dha has a traditional length ranging from three to five feet, and occasionally even longer. Guards on this dha are small, if present at all, and the spine may be smaller than those of Japanese swords (Draeger and Smith,1989; Orwell, 1962). Handles on the Burmese dha are relatively long, with a common blade-to-hilt ratio of two to one (2:1). Shorter dhas are normally meant for single-hand combat applications, despite the long handles. Longer dhas most often require the use of two hands for effective fighting, due to blade weight.

Al Cook executes a trapping technique against the
attacking Terrell LaTour during a short-staff training
session in Athens, Ohio, September 1997.

Bando approaches with the Burmese dha are mostly associated with the various bando animal fighting systems (e.g., panther, eagle, tiger) and the dissuasive tactics of forest monks. Dha training includes many circular patterns of movement with both blade and body. Parrying motions are preferred to blocking in dha defense, with evasive footwork employed to avoid attacks. Offensive skills with the Burmese dha focus on slashing motions that target an opponent's extremities, particularly joints in the arms and legs. Thrusts can focus on body and head targets, yet the primary goal of dha combat is to deliver multiple strikes through continuous body movement. Similar to other traditional weapons, ABA practitioners display dha skills at various martial arts venues throughout the US and abroad (Winborne, 1995).

The Monk System

Martial arts systems have chiefly evolved as highly structured disciplines for delivering destructive techniques for self-defense. Systems throughout Asia and other continents have, for centuries, developed and refined methods designed to hurt, maim, and even kill opponents. Practitioners of these systems are frequently motivated by emotions of pride, fear, anger, dominance, hatred, and vengeance. But there is another overall philosophy that undergirds some martial arts approaches—a philosophy of compassion, healing, and harmonizing. This approach may be usefully defined as the high style or soft system of self-defense. The bando monk system is one such high style in the martial arts (Winborne and Gyi, 1996).

Historians and archaeologists suggest that Brahmin tribes migrated into the Irrawaddy River valley over three thousand years ago and established several kingdoms along this great river. In fact, the name Burma was derived from the Brahmin, who formed a society around 1000 BCE. Several centuries later the peaceful Pyu Kingdom (third to ninth centuries CE) was established within the region of north-central Burma. The Pyu embraced several spiritual beliefs and were known to practice different types of yoga, including raja, karma, tantric, and hatha. The Pyu Kingdom ultimately succumbed to warrior tribes from the north, and many of their writings and symbols were destroyed. The Pyu are, nevertheless, fostering the discipline of forest monks in Burma, who excelled at the practices of meditation, yoga, and self-defense (Gyi, 2000a; Kornfield, 1988).

The most renowned of these forest monks was the Venerable Monk Oopali, who is credited with formalizing the monk system of *thaing* (martial arts) and establishing a religious order during the Great Pagan Era. Oopali's order still exists today in Myanmar, Thailand, Cambodia, and Laos, but his monk system virtually disappeared as a result of successive tribal wars in the region. Only a handful of organizations have attempted to preserve Oopali's legacy. During the nineteenth century, His Holiness Mogok Sayadaw, Mandalay Sayadaw, Mingun Sayadaw, Shwebo Sayadaw, and Amapura Sayadaw were the only elder monks who continued to teach the nonviolent, noncombative, and nonaggressive system of martial arts in northern Burma. Mogok Sayadaw, the supreme abbot of the city of Mogok, was an ardent practitioner of hatha yoga and also a teacher of a nonviolent system of bando. His teachings directly influenced Ba Than Gyi and his son Maung Gyi, resulting in the monk system's continued development in the US.

The monk system is not a religion, a doctrine, or a dogma, even though it is based on ancient Hindu and Buddhist principles of nonviolence. It is a disciplined way of life. It is an integrated system of developing the body, the mind, and the spirit to achieve inner harmony and peaceful coexistence with others. Both empty-hand techniques and weapons are used in monk system self-defense, but the objective is never to maim or to kill. Rather, emphasis is placed on resolving conflicts without the use of violence, since preserving life is given the highest priority (Winborne and Gyi, 1996).

Dr. Maung Gyi offers a lecture to students during a monk camp in Edgewater, Maryland. He holds a traditional monk staff, which is used for self-defense, yoga, and meditation, September 2007.

Three major empty-hand approaches are taught in the monk system. These styles can be studied and practiced independently, or they can be integrated into a comprehensive defensive method. The ghost monk approach is defined as evasive with advanced stepping patterns and body angling that avoid attacks. Parries, blocks, checks, and other shielding methods are combined with the footwork to frustrate an opponent. Cloud monk strategies are designed to control, contain, and restrain opponents (Winborne and Gyi, 1999). Combined with strong, mobile stances, hand movements of the cloud monk will pull, push, and trap an attacker without causing serious injury. The lighting monk approach focuses on nonlethal stunning strikes to specific nerve centers along the body, arms, and legs. Strikes are skillfully applied to avoid vital targets (e.g., eyes, face, throat, etc.), yet these strikes will effectively neutralize opponents without causing permanent injury.

Again, each of the aforementioned empty-hand approaches may be used separately or combined in monk system self-defense. Forest monks of ancient Burma often traveled long distances by foot and carried staffs and ropes during the journey. An advanced system of self-defense naturally evolved from these skillful monks, and many of these techniques are preserved by ABA practitioners. Monk staff methods involve quick strikes to nonvital target areas, similar to the striking methods in the lightning monk approach (Winborne and Gyi, 1997). Constructed from strong bamboo or rattan, the monk staff may be used to trap, push, and throw for effective self-defense. Monk rope techniques may be used to trap, throw, and strike opponents as well. In some instances, the ancient monk in Burma would fashion large knots at the rope's end to create a bolo knot. Skillful striking with the monk rope can readily neutralize opponents, and such techniques are currently practiced by ABA members.

Monk system instructors and students practice a
min zin drill with heavy stones in each hand.
This training method involves deep breathing
and body locking to increase internal power and
physical development, April 2007, Edgewater, Maryland.

There is even an edged-weapon approach within the bando monk system defined as *pongid dha*. This system was also developed and practiced by the ancient Burmese forest monks. Monks who used the pongyi dha devised a system of defense that avoided vital targets and employed the weapon under only the direst circumstances (Gyi, 2000a). When employed, the dha would cut or slash only joint areas of the arms and legs, thereby preserving life. Opponents were not able to continue fighting, yet medical assistance would allow the injured fighter to continue living. Pongyi dha techniques are characterized by circular cutting and shielding patterns, as well as spinning movements of the body. Senior practitioners of the ABA have preserved the pongyi dha system.

Healing methods of the monk system include yoga drills and *min zin*, a comprehensive method for increasing and managing internal energy, to improve physical well-being and to help the body recover from injury or illness. Many yoga drills in the system are similar to those found in India,

Nepal, Thailand, and Tibet (Winborne and Gyi, 1996). Yet there are some unique practices including dhanda yoga, which is performed with a long staff, and longi yoga, which requires a long rope or sturdy cloth. By using a study staff or rope, the practitioner may produce fitness results from yoga not possible without such implements. A method of stretching and restoration involving two persons is also used in the monk system. Specifically, letha yoga sessions involve partner stretches and manipulation to restore the body to optimal functioning.

Dhanda yoga is designed to strengthen the muscles and to align the joints with a long staff. Monk system practitioners are shown performing a sitting dhanda yoga drill at a training camp in Edgewater, Maryland, May 2011.

Min zin is based on written materials from monastic libraries, including those of His Holiness Amarapura Sayadaw (abbot of the Amarapura Monastery, 1860). The practice of min zin in Burma was influenced by the teaching of Venerable Oopali and by theories developed within other Asian cultures. Min zin is a truncated version of a longer Pali phrase refined for easier pronunciation and usage. "*Min*" means king, ruler, conqueror, or controller; "*zin*" means pattern, form, or system (Winborne and Gyi, 1996).

For practical purposes, the term min zin should be understood to mean methods and techniques to cultivate, manage, and express one's internal energy. With similarities to the seven energy centers of hatha yoga, min zin defines nine interconnected areas along the body called chakras that control the body's internal energy flow. Staffs, stones, ropes, beads, and scarfs have been commonly used in traditional min zin practice. There is also a wide range of empty-hand techniques that can be used for energy cultivation. These methods were passed down from ancient Burmese monks.

Duvon Winborne demonstrates the internal power developed
by min zin training. He shatters several coconuts in rapid
succession during a demonstration at the Smithsonian
Institute Folklife Festival in Washington, DC, July 4, 2010.

Summary

Motivated by a strong cultural imperative, U Ba Than Gyi engaged
in an ambitious process during the 1940s to restore ancient combat traditions
of the country currently known as the Republic of the Union of Myanmar.
Many self-defense methods of the Southeast Asian region had existed for
thousands of years, but were largely relegated to obscure practices because
of political upheaval and social changes. The post-World War II period was
critical for Ba Than Gyi's restoration efforts, as principles of the various
fighting methods were systematically gathered and documented. What
resulted was a highly structured amalgam that constituted a modernized
Hanthawaddy bando system.

Ba Than Gyi carefully guided the scholarly and martial development
of his son, Dr. Maung Gyi. Empty-hand approaches, weapons techniques,
grappling strategies, and even a nonviolent self-defense system were taught
to the younger Gyi by his father and other masters. Maung Gyi, in turn,
fostered the growth of Burmese bando on the American continent several
years later. Dr. Gyi founded the American Bando Association (ABA) in
the 1960s, and he introduced full-contact sport fighting to the martial arts
community, along with several other unique approaches.

Presently, there are dozens of highly skilled instructors in the US, trained directly by Maung Gyi. The Burmese system of self-defense has grown substantially since its introduction over fifty years ago. Training seminars and clinics have been sponsored by the ABA in most states and even in neighboring countries, sharing the bando system with a new generation of martial arts students. The survival of the ancient Burmese combat traditions is assured.

Bibliography

Black, J. (Ed.). (2005). *The atlas of world history,* 2nd ed. New York: Dorling Kindersley Inc.

Caplan, L. (2009). *Warrior gentlemen.* Nepal: Himal Books.

Cross, J. P., and Gurung, B. (Eds.). (2002). *In their own words: The Gurkha experience, 1939 to present.* London: Greenhill Books.

Draeger, D. F., and Smith, R. W. (1989). *Comprehensive Asian fighting arts.* New York: Kodansha International/USA Ltd.

Gyi, B. T. (1989). *Manual of the bando discipline.* Atlanta, GA: American Bando Association.

Gyi, M. (2000a). *Bando monk system: Compilation of related articles.* Atlanta, GA: American Bando Association.

Gyi, M. (2000b). *Bando philosophy, principles and practices: An overview of the freehand systems.* Atlanta, GA: American Bando Association.

Hyder, P. F., and Menard, S. D. (1996, November). Bando's eagle soars above the crowd. *Inside Kung-Fu,* 58-61.

Kornfield, J. (1988). *Living Buddhist masters.* Sri Lanka: Buddhist Publication Society.

Kufus, M. (1993, June). The bando bull system. *Black Belt,* 44-46.

Marshall , R. (1993). *Storm from the East: from Genghis Khan to Khubilai Khan.* Berkeley, CA: University of California Press.

Miller, D. E. (1989). A state of grace: Understanding the martial arts. In R. F. Nelson (Ed). *The Overlook martial arts reader* (pp. 143-153). Woodstock, NY: The Overlook Press.

Mitchell, D. (1988). *The Overlook martial arts handbook.* Woodstock, NY: The Overlook Press, 1988.

Nicolle, D. (1990). *The Mongol warlords: Genghis Khan, Kublai Khan, Hulegu, Tamerlane.* New York, NY: Firebird Books.

Orwell, G. (1962). *Burmese days.* New York: Harcourt.

Rai, M., and Kufus, M. (1992, May). "Gorkhali Ayo!" Gurkha soldiers in the battle of Imphal, 1944. *Command*, 52-62.

Rai, M., and Kufus, M. (1994, January). Fighting nature, insects, disease and Japanese: The Chindit War in Burma. *Command*, 22-36.

Rashidi, R., and Van Sertima, I. (Eds). (1985). *African presence in early Asia.* New Brunswick, NJ: Transaction Publishers.

Scherban, D., and Nightingale, C. H. (1986, October). Achieving skin like steel: Take a licking and keep on kicking. *Inside Kung-Fu*, 52-55.

Winborne, D. G. (1994, May). The bando scorpion style: A natural lesson. *Inside Kung-Fu*, 70-72, 90.

Winborne, D. G. (1995, December). Burmese bando: Fighting reduced to its functional essence. *Inside Kung-Fu*, 14-23.

Winborne, D. G. (1996, May). Bando's khukuri: A sword for combat, survival and ceremony. *Inside Kung-Fu*, 72-77.

Winborne, D. G. (2011). *The Burmese warrior spirit: 40 years of bando boxing in America.* Atlanta, GA: American Bando Association.

Winborne, D. G., and Anderson, S. (2000, March). The eye of the cobra. *Inside Kung-Fu*, 54-57, 84-93.

Winborne, D. G., and Gyi, M. (1995, March). Throws to blows to holds: Shifting trends in martial arts. *Martial Arts Ultimate Warriors*, 42-47.

Winborne, D. G., and Gyi, M. (1996, December). Making peace with yourself: A non-violent approach to a violent art. *Inside Kung-Fu*, 70-72, 90.

Winborne, D. G., and Gyi, M. (1997, June). Training with bando's long staff. *Inside Kung-Fu*, 42-45, 78-79.

Winborne, D. G., and Gyi, M. (1997, July). First bando monk seminar challenges the spirit. *Inside Kung-Fu*, 122.

Winborne, D. G., and Gyi, M. (1999, October). Bando evasion skills: Art of not being there. *Black Belt*, 48-53, 164-165.

index

Made in the USA
Coppell, TX
17 July 2021

59090514R00055